Praise for Colin Turner's work

'Truly inspiring. I doubt whether anyone's life will remain unchanged after reading it' *Here's Health*

'What Colin Turner writes is worth reading' *Business Age*

'Creates positive results' *Evening Standard*

'Highly recommended' *Financial Times*

'Sound Advice' *Daily Mail*

'Crammed full of seriously good advice' *The Irish News*

'Turner preaches what he has practised' *Sunday Independent*

'The thinking person's Little Book of Calm' *Belfast Telegraph*

'Highly researched yet intuitive'
N. Holloway MD, Microsoft UK

'East meets West for success' *His Excellency, Ma Zengang*

'Colin's philosophy works' *C. Cowdray, CEO, Claridges*

'Compulsory reading' *Dr Marilyn Orcharton, Founder, Denplan*

'An excellent blueprint for success' *Sir Michael Grylls*

'The philosophy for the 21st Century'
Vera Peiffer, 'Positive Thinking'

'Timeless Wisdom' *Kyodo News*

'A source of inspiration – read it!' *BBC*

The

Teachings

of

Billionaire

Yen Tzu

**21st
Century
Books**

The Teachings of Billionaire Yen Tzu

Volume 1

Published in Great Britain in 2004 by
21st Century Books UK Limited
30 Queen Square, Bristol, BS1 4ND
www.21stcenturybooks.uk.com
service@21stcenturybooks.uk.com

Cover Design by Dick Evry, Bath
Printed and bound in the UK by Antony Rowe Ltd,
Chippenham, Wilts

British Library Cataloguing in Publication
Data available

ISBN: 1-904956-01-7

The

Teachings

of

Billionaire

Y e n T z u

V
O
L
U
M
E

I

infinite patience; immediate results

Contents

Author's Note

There is a legend that tells of a famous Academy, now lost in the mountains of an Eastern Province. Founded some two and a half millennia ago by an immensely successful Patriarch, *Yen Tzu*, the School attracted the interest of great leaders, merchants, and individuals, from all over the ancient world; earnestly seeking the secrets of a new alchemy proven to deliver prosperity and well-being.

Possibly a member of the inner circle of Taoist Sages, *Yen Tzu* would have been fully versed in the Metaphysical Wisdom of the Ancients. His paradoxical philosophy, therefore, would have certainly followed the way of self-mastery through individual inner understanding.

Over several generations the School's acclaim grew through word of mouth, as each student, enlightened by their understanding of this new thinking, graduated. Such a level of understanding was certainly instrumental in *Yen Tzu* becoming Ancient China's first commercial billionaire; though such success inevitably attracted the attention of an aspiring Emperor.

History records that in the year 213BCE almost all remnants of this ancient teaching were destroyed by the first Emperor of what we now consider to be geographical China: the ruthless Qin Shi Huang, famous for the army of life-size Terracotta Warriors guarding his mausoleum; unearthed in Lintong County, Shaanxi.

Viewing such teaching as a threat to the divine rule he had decreed, he was convinced that by destroying it no-one would question or usurp his dictatorship. Pursuing this policy to control society's thinking, his brutal Prime Minister, Li Ssu, ordered countless sages to be executed and their places of learning to be burned to the ground. In an attempt to save them from destruction, valuable scrolls and texts were hidden in hollowed walls, a time-honoured custom utilised by numerous cultures over the ages.

History records that the Qin Dynasty lasted only during his lifetime, a mere forty-one years; a vivid reminder that motives seeking manipulation and control are always short-lived. Unwittingly, Qin had destroyed the very wisdom that could have been his greatest strength as a leader.

Yet, today, in the 21st Century and despite the immense power at our fingertips, the majority of businesses survive a few years and most people retire with little money. Clearly the application of a new thinking and practice is as valid now as it was to prosperity over two millennia ago.

Though there is growing awareness in the Western world of the danger of being enslaved to mindless consumption – indeed most of us prefer sustainable quality over disposable quantity – we continue to suffer on many counts. The labels of *me, my* and *mine* impose artificial limitations on the enjoyment of our life; and worrying over our status and what we can solicit from others prevents us from being true to ourselves.

There are many delusions to be cleared and the thought-provoking lessons taught by forgotten sages and harnessed by great leaders and merchants are revealed within this book. Although these revelations shake the pillars of current thinking, they uncannily strike deep chords within us, because of the sound truths that resonate from them. For achieving self-mastery through individual inner understanding is the only sure and timeless way to fully develop our potential, achieve our purpose and ensure our spiritual growth.

Paradoxically, through their initial obscurity, the answers currently sought by our modern world appear. Work can no longer be viewed as a separate compartment to the way we live our lives, either personally or professionally. With the increasing demand for a practical philosophy for meaningful, purposeful and sustainable success, my own research and hands-on studies led to me writing these two volumes. In doing so, I sought to unlock and share esoteric secrets and explain forgotten truths in the form of twelve lessons. They encapsulate through parables my interpretation of the genre of ancient wisdom, as taught by *Yen Tzu*.

By reading these volumes that comprise *The Teachings of Yen Tzu,* you will begin to perceive opportunities to test the potency of the ideas they contain. In this way you will become a graduate of self-mastery.

Colin Turner

Taming the Bull

Harmonising Communication

'*oeless Wong was crippled for allowing Duke Ling's prize bull to run amok in the kilns,*' said Ho Chi, in answer to his fellow disciple's question. '*Indeed, it is said, that he lost a toe for every one of the ten Imperial vases that were smashed.*'

'*In truth it was through having his feet stamped on by the mighty bull while he bravely fought to recapture it,*' said their Patriarch, upon overhearing their discourse.

'*By my ancestors,*' exclaimed Ho Chi, '*what courage!*'

'*Indeed yes,*' said Yen Tzu, '*but fighting yang with yang is not the way to communicate and overcome.*'

'*It is said that yin and yang connect all,*' said Ho Chi, '*but please explain how, in the context of such a difficult situation.*'

'*The mutual seeking of yin and yang depends on opening and closing.*' began the Patriarch. '*Opening and closing are the natural principles that influence the rise and fall in all of heaven and earth's ten thousand things, including man and beast. Yin and yang should always be harmonious. For the opposite of one, redresses the balances of the other.*'

'*When the bull was in yang mode, so was Toeless Wong. Rather than adopting yin mode, he fought charge with charge.*'

He pitted his aggression against the bull's aggression. When yang is hard and aggressive, only the yielding softness of yin can calm it. As a seasoned keeper, Wong knew full well how to calm the bull. But seeing the crashing commotion before him he forgot, and was as a fool rushing in. In doing so, he was no different to the bull.

'Yin and yang modes can be taught to be switched on or off according to what is needed. Yin or yang must be used as appropriate to tame that part within all of us which can be likened to a charging bull, and to soften the raging bull within others who appear to be attacking us. Men do not mirror themselves in running water; they can only see themselves in still water. Only what is still, can calm to stillness others.

'Always remember that it is important to know when to speak and when to remain silent. When you want to hear others' voices, return to silence; when you want to be expansive, be withdrawn; when you want to rise, lower yourself; when you want to take, give; and when you want to overcome, give way.'

❧ All through school we're taught to read, write and speak, but apart from how to listen critically, we are never taught to really communicate. Yet the way in which we communicate inwardly and outwardly directly influences the quality of our relationships with others, as well as with ourselves. True communication, however, goes way beyond our variety of listening skills learned through tuition.

❧ All of us have a dormant bull within us, desperate to be heard and we usually allow another person to turn it loose.

Those people who are prone to argue, will claim that any heated intercourse, be it debate, discussion or family tiff, requires such stimulation. Healthy arguments making for healthy relationships is a myth, however, as when two people allow themselves to become angry towards each other, there are two losers. In the same way that it is pointless to fight fire with fire, being angry with others burns our valuable psychic body into a charred shell.

✔ Understanding the nature of how things interact helps us to harmonise those universal forces that can then strengthen us, instead of allowing an imbalance which hurts us. The very nature of communicating with ourselves through listening to our inner world, for example, reflects directly on our interpersonal communication with others. The principle for listening is the same as evaluation. You cannot evaluate others until you have successfully evaluated yourself; and you cannot effectively listen externally until you have mastered listening internally.

✔ What is not said can be clearly audible in our inner stillness, and what is not said is more valuable to us than whatever is being said. Through inward and outward stillness we become able to listen to others without influencing what they say by our reactions. For example, the speech of others is yang movement, for it is outward; one's own silence is yin stillness, for it is receptive. When the statements of another are inconsistent, if we reflect and enquire introspectively, then an appropriate response will be forthcoming.

9

✦ To use stillness to listen to what is being voiced, means exercising our ability to look at matters from all angles, without entertaining any associations or attachments that may affect our understanding. Yang is opening up, yin is closing down. Opening up involves assessing people's feelings, closing down involves making sure of their sincerity, and not believing that we must get our point in first, particularly during an argument.

✦ Learning to communicate *fully* instead of having to manipulate *partly* when we are with others, means being ourselves. Without doubt that is the first and most important step in effective communication. But it also means harmonising yin and yang so that our inner and outer worlds remain balanced.

Emptying Fullness

'Give us a tale, honourable sir,' said Ho Chi, 'as to how Man can know when to be silent and when to speak.'

'Silence and speaking relate to the emptiness and fullness of Man,' began Yen Tzu. 'If your mind is filled with your own prejudices, the truth that others speak cannot be heard. When engaging in conversation, most people are in a hurry to express their own opinion. As a result they don't hear anything but the sound of their own voices.

'Imagine a man, with his hull full of stores, crossing the Yellow River,' continued the Patriarch, 'and an empty boat *happens along and bumps into him. No matter how hot-tempered the man may be, he will not get angry. But, if there should be someone in the other boat, then he will shout out to them to haul this way or veer that. If his first shout is unheeded, he will shout out again, and if that is not heard, he will shout a third time, this time accompanied with a torrent of curses. In the first instance, he wasn't angry; in the second he is. Earlier he faced emptiness, now he faces occupancy. When he is faced with occupancy he allows the dialogue of his fullness to take over: how he considers the state of things should be. If a man could succeed in making himself empty, and in that way wander through the world, then who could do him harm?'*

'But Man seems to always want to speak more to blame than to praise, regardless of what he brings on himself,' said Ho Chi.

'Exactly so! Which is why one must learn to speak sparingly,' added Yen Tzu. 'A word is a bird. Once let out, you can't whistle it back. Measure your words. Think that every word is a coin and once it goes out, it won't return. For in certainty speech is priceless if you speak with knowledge. As such it must be weighed in the scales of the heart, before it comes from the mouth.'

¥ Through the process of listening to others a large percentage of our hearing is overrun by a constant evaluation of the incoming messages we are receiving. 'What does he think he is doing? Do I agree with this or that? Why are they saying this or that? Why don't they make their point? What is it that happened to me that is similar? Why doesn't she let me get a word in? That tie doesn't suit them', and so on. We literally hold two questions at once. Constant internal chatter creates a 'fullness' where an 'emptiness' is required.

❧ Where is the usefulness in a vase for flowers? It is in the empty space that receives them and not the pleasant external facade. As we would feel the mood of an empty house, we can learn to see the emptiness. When a group of people sit in a circle, either around a board table or in any meeting, it is the climate or the spirit in the centre – the empty space – that determines the nature of the group's atmosphere. The fruitfulness of a meeting, for example, can be clearly determined by the atmosphere during the silences. The difficulty is that meetings, particularly in the West, are not considered to be about silences. Indeed any pauses in some meetings are simply seen as opportunities to either drive points home or as a signal that the meeting is terminated.

❧ It is because of the non-ownership of what results from a meeting that further meetings are then often planned. The business world, for example, is full of meetings where, although the *atmosphere* of it may not be heeded at the time, whatever is perceived from such an atmosphere is soon discussed afterwards in the privacy of quiet corners. In the same way that we refuse to hear our higher-self whispering to us in the silent gap between our thoughts, due to our internal dialogue, we miss important elements of what is being related to us by others. Then, whatever we do miss, we tend to compensate with our own interpretations of what we think others said.

✻ As infinitely more is communicated by what is not said than by words alone, it is important to listen to the empty parts or silence. Conditioning in the Western world has taught us to be uncomfortable with silences during an active conversation. Silent communication is something that inscrutable Eastern sages engaged in as a matter of course. They would remain silent *after* the person they were talking to had finished speaking, in order to listen to what they were hearing within as well as without. Although common in psychotherapy, modern Man generally prefers to prepare his reply *before* the person he is speaking to has finished. His internal dialogue is amplified when what is being said strongly opposes the listener's own point of view.

✻ This is because most of us tend to believe that listening means listening *critically*. In searching for what we agree with or, more predominantly, disagree with, we feel we are paying attention. Indeed many people only feel that they are offering worthwhile support when they are pointing out the flaw in an argument. But bearing in mind that they prepare their answer based on their own opinions drawn from their own circumstances and based on their own frame of reference, the proverbial 'baby' of an idea can be often drowned in their full, overflowing 'bath'. There is nothing wrong with pointing out a flaw, except when the whole focus of attention is on doing so.

✻ As our tendency is to listen to others within the boundaries of our own experience, we keep strengthening the root of most communication problems. Because we see the world as we are, not as it is, we find it hard to listen with empathy. Clever listening skills may have taught us to keep quiet while the other person is talking, but most of the time our listening is tuned to something we want to hear, something that is useful to us, or someone we want to impress, sell to or gain something from.

𝖞 This fairly cynical view is because the majority of us are only interested in improving our communication skills to further our own interests, in other words – 'what's in it for me?' To have empathy means to empty ourselves of any hidden agenda whatsoever. It means moving into the hearts and minds of others to genuinely begin to see the world as they see it, not as we think they should see it. Often, when talking with another we are itching to get our point over as to how to sort out a problem, by relating how we sorted out a similar one.

𝖞 Our conditioning has further taught us to believe that we must get our point in first, particularly during an argument. The way we see it is all that matters to us. We believe that taking the time to listen to another while not defending, attacking, or judging, conveys acquiescence and agreement with their viewpoint. In thinking that listening to others in order to understand their feelings denotes weakness we are communicating predominantly in the full yang mode. To develop the receptive, yin, mode we need to be calm ourselves. In this way we can listen to people, assess the myriad of things that they want to say, measure their abilities and see into their intentions clearly without misunderstanding.

✢ It is indeed amazing that one of the world's largest and most lucrative professions, law, has developed because people are unable to resolve their disputes through their own communication. This would certainly seem to be a fact of our conditioned life that is now well and truly entrenched within our culture. Man will generally look to blame, instead of looking for the solution, in the same manner that he will spend more time getting out of something than getting on with it.

✢ It is certainly worth asking ourselves how much of our time and energy is wasted in some kind of defensive or protective communication, internal squabbling, inter-departmental backbiting, politics and interpersonal disputes. Then if we take the time to pick any one of those disputes or arguments that come to mind, it is worth asking ourselves if we are capable of resolving the situation without external assistance.

✢ Admittedly, there are these irritating situations when one is dealing with faceless adversaries, such as the computer which may be 'down at the moment'. But generally if we empty ourselves of our hidden agendas a solution can be reached. The fact is that when we take the time to shut down during a conversation, we know how to resolve it. The aphorism of 'least said soonest mended', however, is too often not considered when communicating. Instead we prefer to issue advice, or take issue with what we believe is being said.

Silence is Golden

There was once a loyal servant who worked for a wise counsellor. Each day different people would visit and pay handsomely for the advice they sought. After ten years of working hard without asking for wages, receiving just bed and board, the servant declared his intent to return to his home village. Asked for all the wages that were due, the wise counsellor was pleased to give his servant the enormous sum of two hundred gold crowns, for his ten years of service.

But just as the servant was about to leave his master asked him if, after all these years of showing people into the house who sought counsel, he was going to depart without hearing a word of advice. Not wanting to offend his former master, the man agreed.

'Excellent! I have two valuable pieces of advice but you must pay me my usual rate of course – one hundred crowns for each nugget!'

The former servant paled as he accepted the terms.

'Right,' said the master, 'you are listening attentively aren't you?'

'Yes I am most certainly listening,' replied the servant.

'Excellent! Now, always remember: Don't interfere in the affairs of others. Live and let live.'

'Live and let live!' exclaimed the servant. 'Why I could have

heard that from the town gipsy for half a crown!'

'Ah, but at this price you will be sure to heed it,' came the reply.

The servant applied all the loyalty of ten years to hold back from saying what he really thought. Pushing the bag containing two hundred crowns towards his master while shaking his head in disbelief, he said through gritted teeth 'And the second piece?'

'Always remember,' said the counsellor, looking deeply into the eyes of his faithful servant, 'to save your anger until the following day. Always review in the light of dawn.'

As the servant shook his head in incredulity, his former master said, 'Now then, I can't let you leave with nothing. Here is a special cake I have had prepared so you can celebrate upon your return home.'

Taking the heavy cake, without as much as a glance, the servant dumbly thanked the old man and set off on his journey. Inside he was both aching with disappointment and frustration, thinking how wasted his ten years had been.

After a few days' travelling the servant entered a forest. As daylight began to fade he began to feel uneasy. Eventually walking in almost total darkness along the narrowing road, it was with relief that he glimpsed a light ahead. But as he approached a woodsman hut window from whence the light came he felt a huge wave of uneasiness. Tired and disoriented he ignored the feeling and knocked. A huge ox of a man opened the door. The servant had to stifle an involuntary cry as he gazed into the most terrifying face he had ever encountered.

The servant's grim host motioned to him to sit at the table and began to ladle out soup. To the servant's astonishment not *a word was spoken. Hungry from his journey he was soon finishing his bowl when a barely audible knock from under the floor made him start. His host snorting like a bull lowered his huge arm down and pulled open a hatch on the floor. The servant was mortified to witness the surfacing of an emaciated woman dressed in filthy rags, deep empty sockets in her face where her eyes should have been. The servant watched, dumbstruck, as his host reached up to the shelf for a human skull, turned it upside down, ladled the now cold soup into and pushed a dirty drinking straw into one of the eye holes. After making the woman drink through it he roughly pushed her back into her subterranean prison, slammed the hatch tightly shut and then quickly turned toward his guest.*

'Well traveller, what do you think of that!'

'I'll tell you just what I think,' said the servant about to give the man a piece of his mind. But just as suddenly he distinctly heard his former master's advice: "Don't interfere in the affairs of others. Live and let live." The servant bit his tongue and said: 'I think that you must have a very good reason for your actions.'

The bull of a man seemed surprised. 'I do! That creature you glimpsed was my wife. Years ago I caught her with her lover...both tried to kill me! That is his skull she uses as her soup bowl. I will never forgive, but who knows I might forget. So, what do you think of what I have done!'

'I think that you did the only thing you knew how to do,' answered the servant.

'You are by far the wisest visitor ever to have survived my hospitality. All who have disagreed with me lay deeply buried; their throats cut.

As the bull of a man showed him where he could sleep the servant's mouth was so dry it was hard to swallow. Hoarsely he replied a goodnight to his host. Lying in his bed he was astounded at what he has seen and how the words of his former master had saved his life.

Having departed early the next morning, the servant continued until he at last began to recognise familiar landmarks. The dull ache of fear left him as excitement at being with his family grew within him. Despite hurrying, it was late when he spotted with joy the welcoming light from his home. Through the window he immediately recognised his wife and was overcome with emotion. Then, through his tears, he saw that there was a group of other people in the room. Then, to his dismay he saw a man walk towards his wife and embrace her. Everyone in the room began to clap as the two people kissed, laughed and began to dance.

The servant's dismay grew quickly to an infuriated rage. 'So it has been a long time, but you could not wait for me – or would not. Taking another, in my home! I'll kill him! I'll kill both of you!' Unsheathing the knife he carried on his belt he prepared to rush at them. Just at the moment when he was about to leap through the window he hesitated, hearing his old master's words ringing in his ears: "Save your anger until the following day – review in the light of dawn."

Never before had he exerted so much effort over controlling himself. Forcing his shaking hand to sheath the dagger, he growled to himself, 'All right I will save my anger until the following day, but only until then!' He then ran back into the woods to spend a restless night, determined to satisfy his honour the following day.

Not falling asleep until dawn, he awoke mid-morning and began to walk briskly through the village. As he did so he came across an old neighbour friend who recognised him.

'After all these years I don't believe it!' said the neighbour as he embraced his friend. 'And what a time to return just as your son has graduated from the House of Scholars. His mother was so happy; she danced half the night with him.'

'By the gods!' said the servant, shocked that in the heat of the moment he had almost killed his own son and wife. 'My master's words were indeed worth everything I had.'

Rushing up to his home there was at first shocked surprise as the door opened, followed by tears of joy and cries of welcome. As his family shouted for more celebrations, the servant remembered the gift from his former master.

'I have the perfect thing!' he said, and lifted the heavy cake out of his bag and on to the table. Using the same knife he had unsheathed the night before in anger, the servant cut through it and pulled out the first slice. As he did so, golden coins began to roll out all over the place. Bewildered and excited everyone sprang to collect it. Upon counting the gold it came to two hundred crowns.

✱ The true worth of advice can never be fully appreciated unless it is well paid for. Indeed the propensity to ignore good advice is in direct proportion to the frequency it is freely given. When advice comes free it is never valued and seldom heeded. In giving all his wages for his master's advice, the servant naturally felt he had been cheated. But because the advice had cost him so dear, he remembered and heeded it.

✶ There is a far deeper meaning, however, with regard to his application of the first piece of advice. The intuitive, feminine or yin part of us, so vital in making our own decisions, is very often kept repressed, abused and imprisoned underground, a tortured representation of our locked up feelings. We instead ask for the free advice and opinions of others, who are as free with their advice as to what we should do, as we are with our advice to them.

✶ When we suggest something that is not what people want to hear, they can, metaphorically speaking, go for our throat, killing off our worth, and burying us in the back of their minds as one of the reasons they have their problem. The best form of advice is in itself a valuable listening method and is applied by all leaders and achievers, who realise that as we have two ears and one mouth it is best to use them in that order. It is simply: 'What do *you* think you should do?' That way people come up with their own solution, leave satisfied, and thank you.

✶ The importance of keeping our own counsel and trusting to our intuition during our interpersonal communications is paramount to harmonising yin and yang. Without them we are at constant risk of jumping to conclusions in all areas of our lives. Before asking advice of others, ask yourself if you are prepared to pay for it. Upon receiving it, ask yourself if you truly value the worth that you were prepared to pay for it. Then observe if, when the occasion arises, you ignore or heed the advice.

✔ Become aware of listening to your own advice, seeing if you really have the courage of your own convictions. Observe also if you are a person who prejudges situations without fully investigating the fact. Observe also if you have a tendency to suggest to others what they ought to do. Then, if you become aware that you have this tendency, notice how you are actually the one that suffers most of all. Next time you have the urge or compulsion to raise questions, or argue a point someone is making, practice holding your tongue and instead listen to what is really being said. You will discover a communication that is far more satisfactory than the outer discussions and arguments of people who know not what they discuss.

✔ When you are able to practise these elements in your daily interactions with others, you will be well on the way to understanding the natural flow of communication. To learn the skills of effective communication means following the 'sowing before reaping' principle – listening before speaking. Where the mouth is the mechanism, the ears and the eyes are the assistants of the heart and mind. When these three respond in harmony, they act in a beneficial way. To listen primarily with the eyes and heart and secondarily with ears, means listening on four levels: physical, emotional, mental and spiritual. When used in harmony, all levels allow us to hear what is really being said, rather than merely hearing superficially.

✔ When we first hear something, we hear it on the physical level. We hear the actual words, the softness or loudness created by the vibration of speaking. Then we hear the feeling, belief and enthusiasm at the emotional level. At the mental level we notice what is important to us. Much of our schooling ensured that we hear well at this level. At the spiritual level what we hear wakes us up to what we already know; we may not fully understand what is being said, but something tells us that it makes sense.

✱ Whenever we are playing a role and not being ourselves, it is not possible to hear on all four levels because our attention is diverted. It is diverted to ensure that our role is not discovered by the person we are communicating with. We are not usually aware of this, as it is an automatic response, but it has a dramatic effect on our ability to listen. Ask yourself, 'Do people communicate by what they say, or by how they really feel about what they say?'

Never Explain, Never Complain

In a small temple lost in the mountains, four pupil monks were practising Zazen. They agreed amongst themselves to observe seven days of silence. The first day of meditation began auspiciously but, as night began to fall, one of the monks began to feel annoyed that the lamps were not being lit.

'It was your turn to light the lamps,' he complained to one of his colleagues.

The second monk was surprised to hear the first one talk. 'In my concentration of not speaking I forgot,' he explained.

'Listen to you two,' said the third pupil, 'Why did you talk?'

'I am the only one who has not talked,' concluded the fourth.

⸎ Most of us find it hard to remain silent, even when we have promised ourselves to watch what we say. The degree that we are externally influenced, rather than internally motivated, is in direct proportion to our need to complain about things or explain ourselves to others. Consider how much of your daily communication, for example, is taken up with explaining yourself. The cause is partly our deep-rooted blame culture and partly because we are concerned about how we appear to others.

⸎ Human beings prefer to live by echoes rather than by silence, as when hearing none, they feel insecure. A man may invent an idea of himself as being pleasant, dynamic or popular, or unapproachable, stern or difficult. He then broadcasts his idea of himself to the surrounding world. While preferring an agreeable echo from others, he will also accept a critical one, for anything is better than hearing nothing. When we learn to live without needing the echoes of others to confirm our belief in ourselves, we no longer experience fearful dependency on others.

⸎ The fact is that whatever anyone thinks of us, it is none of our business. This is a strong statement, and should not to be misconstrued as an edict to be irresponsible towards others or ourselves. In all principles the Golden Rule of do unto others what you would have done unto yourself, stands firm. But we cannot know what goes on in the depth of someone else's mind, or heart, from moment to moment as well as they do. Nor can they know exactly how we feel from moment to moment. Infinite combinations of conditioned experiences create unique frames of reference for each of us, even though there is universal connectedness. It is therefore impossible to try and keep everyone happy all of the time. Only by becoming entirely unconcerned about what others *choose* to think of us from *their* frame of reference, are we on the path to becoming our own person.

✝ It is worth remembering that at any one time we are either in control of ourselves, or being controlled by another. There is no neutral. A person can quite easily give up control, for example, by inventing the self-image of being a desirable person, which others can then control through flattery. But what can others control if the person is comfortable in just being themselves?

✝ The fact is that we communicate more about ourselves in the moment before we speak, than in the ten moments that follow. We cannot fail to communicate clearly to another, even without words, particularly when that person is attuned to what is *really* being communicated. This is because meanings are not found in words, they are found in people.

✝ What is communicated in the moment before we speak? Trust, confidence, sincerity and compassion; *or* distrust, nervousness, insincerity or thoughtlessness. When there is trust and confidence we can almost communicate without words. When trust is lacking, communication is exhausting and ineffective. Trust and confidence need to be communicated first; because people don't care how much you know, until they know how much you care.

❧ With improved communication being high on the agenda of businesses anxious to reduce manipulation, departmental rivalry, contest and positioning, political backbiting and destructive gossip, many personnel understandably attend courses. These initiatives, which focus on listening skills and team-building, are well intentioned, but their effects are often short-lived because they seldom pay attention to the lack of self-trust people feel. Self-trust is the basis of trust towards others, which is in turn the very basis of effective communication.

❧ When we learn to know and understand ourselves, we begin to trust ourselves. When we begin to have confidence in our own feelings and act on them, we are becoming self-reliant. When we are self-reliant and enjoy this self-trust, we no longer worry what others say about us because we are increasingly our own person.

❧ Such a pathway naturally leads to less negative complaining. Whenever we are not satisfied with how we genuinely believe things should be, any form of constructive complaining can be applied in a positive light. But the majority of our daily complaints do not relate to this. We allow our powers of communication to be occupied by trivia, obsessed by how things *should* be.

❧ Most of the time we complain out of habit, a habit that weakens us, literally draining us of our positive energy. Yet we are all conscious of doing it. Like the four pupil monks, we unwittingly compromise our good intentions by the need to complain about what others should, or should not be doing, and the need to explain to others why we did or did not do something. With our entrenched habit of 'putting people straight' and constant invitations to 'explain yourself', it is of course difficult to spend just one day with good intentions, let alone a week. But taking one day to consciously not explain or complain will show how significantly different we can feel.

⽑ Without doubt, our quality of life is determined by the quality of our relationships. They provide us with our greatest joy and our deepest sorrow. The less we complain and explain, the more sincere we become. When we become sincere with others, openness and trust builds and communication is developed with or without words.

Balanced Worth

⽑ We cannot communicate more than we are, so it follows that we must seek to understand ourselves in order to recognise who others are. This requires learning to listen to our self, rather than the roles we adopt in order to please everybody. We need to understand that communication is infinitely more than simply words; it is the ability to transmit ourselves successfully to others and receive their thoughts and feelings.

⽑ For how we truly express ourselves is the manifestation of how we each individually think and feel. This means acknowledging that we communicate much more by our silence than by our speech. In doing so we begin to harmonise the yin and yang of communication, instead of allowing our yang, outward movement, of speech to dominate, thus causing us to miss so much of what is really being communicated.

🜂 In feeling the need to offer advice as freely as we may have previously done, we need to accept that communication must be unconditional. To truly listen to another requires us to empty ourselves of our assumptions, prejudices and opinions that each of us carries around, waiting for an opportunity to use. This in turn involves knowing our own position, by questioning our beliefs in order to understand how they may distort our communication with others.

🜂 In this way we can learn to appreciate where others are coming from. For, without doubt, the secret central to good communication is making the person you are talking to feel valued, without compromising your own worth. To do so successfully is to balance the yin and yang of communication as described within this lesson. For only when both are working in harmony is it possible to tame the bull within you and calm the bull within others.

Freeing the Bear

Growing Strong Relationships

*K*ung was alarmed to hear the husky growl that awoke him. Even with the shortcut he had taken to C'hu it was an arduous five-day journey, so that when he found a tranquil spot in which to camp he had fallen asleep almost immediately.

'By the gods!' he exclaimed, 'what devil is that?' as the angry roar continued. Adrenaline soothed his immediate panic as he braved himself to investigate further. It seemed that the roar was not approaching; rather it was changing to one of a crying roar. His search led him to a clearing where he saw an enormous bear caught in a vicious bamboo trap.

Fearing for his life his immediate thought was to flee, but upon hearing the bear now whimper, he stopped in his tracks. Summoning up all of his courage, he began to speak consolingly to the bear and noticed that the bear's big brown eyes were full of pleading.

What he did next, however, would make him wonder for many years what had ever possessed him to do so. Perhaps it was because the creature seemed to sense his genuine compassion, that it allowed Kung to get close enough to remove the trap. Immediately he had, the speed of the bear took his breath away. In an instant the bear held him in a life threatening hug. Expecting his body to be crushed at any moment and torn limb from limb, Kung momentarily realised how mad he had been. Then just as quickly, the animal released him, sniffed him, and limped across the clearing and disappeared into the heavy foliage. Kung, however, saw the bear's eyes in his dreams for many weeks, for it had been thanking him, not hurting him.

Ten years later, Kung was visiting C'hu where his cousins had a surprise for him. 'From your old story, cousin, we know how you like to fight bears!' they teased. 'Come, we are going to see Keeper Lok who is visiting with his bear show.'

Kung was appalled at the state of the mistreated creatures which had obviously been whipped into submission. During the show, one of the larger bears suddenly raised itself to its full height and sniffed the air, as if recognising something. As it did so, Keeper Lok viciously pulled on the chain running through its nose ring causing it to roar with pain. Perhaps because the beast could no longer take such injustice to itself, it drew on its final spirit and with an enormous growl from its now toothless mouth, tore itself free. With blood spurting from its ripped nose it rushed at its cruel keeper, squeezing the life out of him in seconds.

While the mesmerised crowd panicked, Kung stood absolutely still. The eyes that had already searched him out were not pleading to him this time, they were thanking him. Having recognised Kung's scent, the bear had gained the courage to free itself this time. Within moments the great bear had lumbered away seeking its escape.

Kung knew in his mind that the bear's freedom would be short-lived, that it would be hunted, caught and destroyed. But *in his heart he knew that the unconditional service he had performed for the bear had atoned for the seemingly malicious ways of Mankind in the eyes of the bear. The bear had never forgotten him and taken strength from his kind act of long ago. Since that day Kung himself had made a habit of providing unconditional service towards others, despite their growling. Since that day he had never been afraid, nor considered it a weakness, to show kindness or serve another.*

The experience had taught him, above anything else, that with all relationships there was risk; but it was a risk worth taking. In the last ten years he had met with peasants, dukes and marquises. He had even conversed with the Emperor. But all of them he had looked upon the same in his heart, knowing that every person was a living creature that had the right to be treated equally, regardless of their station.

Most of us are unable to free ourselves from our hidden agendas of insecurities, anxieties, desires and hopes, particularly in the work arena. Because of this we are more reserved, shy, suspicious and cynical towards others we meet for the first time, than we are relaxed, confident, and open. Apart from the hugs we dutifully give relatives in appreciation of their annual gifts, we are basically backward in coming forward in respect of our affections towards others.

We reserve our warmth and affection for those who are very close to us, with reserve being the operative word, for even then we never consider being *too* demonstrative. After all, it isn't the done thing. How is it possible, therefore, to focus on being customer-oriented and develop strategy to build long-term relationships, when we can't often be spontaneous even with those we love?

✯ The fact is that our lives are given true value for what we do for others and our relationships with them, not by our relationships with our possessions, our accomplishments and our careers. These are only valuable when they serve as a vehicle to enhance our relationship with ourselves and other people. Increasingly, in our heavily biased commercial society, we have placed things and accomplishments above people.

✯ By understanding that absolutely no-one is in our life by accident, we can begin to accept that human relationships are part of why we live, as only through them can we grow and awaken. Some people offer us larger lessons than others, giving us the opportunity to become more tolerant, accepting, understanding and, ultimately, loving.

✯ Given that a primary purpose for life involves the fulfilling of our potential, it is clear that we can only achieve that purpose with the help of others. Regardless of how much a Man, through his self-sufficiency, considers himself to be an island, he can only be fully developed and realise his full potential through help, support, belief and love. But how much do we truly value others?

✯ The more we value something, the more we devote our time and attention to it. We must ask ourselves, therefore, what message we are sending to our children, spouse, family and friends when we spend fifty to seventy hours a week in our work-place, and only a few hours with them. Of course we love them, but the clear signal is that we fear failing more in our businesses, than we do in our family.

In the work arena people are increasingly aware of the truism that customers don't buy companies or products, they buy people. However, the clear signal sent to the customer is continuously at odds with this. In the same way that people will be more interested to see their own image on holiday photos, family or conference videos, customers are more interested in getting what they want, rather than in helping a company grow. Yet they are still treated as a means to an end and they know it. Most companies do not know how to be customer focused, or build long-term relationships, because the majority of people do not know how to serve. The only way to serve is to *want* to serve. But how many really can do this, when the belief that serving others is tantamount to being servile is so entrenched?

People will not generally help others unless there is something in it for them. Indeed it is so rare, that when it happens it can become headline news. In showing interest to buy from a commission-only salesperson, he or she begins to warm to us. When that interest does not spark, there is coolness towards us. When we do receive good service from others it really does make our day and we tell the world about it because it is so rare and unexpected.

✔ Without question, the ability to provide unconditional service towards others is the key requirement for success in business and in life. This means knowing how, and wanting, to develop strong relationships regardless of outcome. It is important, therefore, to define service, unconditional service and a strong relationship. In going to collect our car after its service, we find it finished. All the points, which we drew the service department's attention to, have been dealt with as expected and the cost is just what we anticipated. The man behind the counter is busy, but takes the time for us and is reasonably polite, as expected. This is good, but this is *not* service.

✔ Service is doing the unexpected. When we return to find that the car has had a full valet, with a letter or gift on the seat thanking us for our custom; or when the assistant takes the time to treat us like the most important person in the world by being genuinely pleased to have served us; and asks us if there is anything else they can do for us, including collecting or delivering our car for us next time, we feel 'Wow! This is great', as a chore has been turned into something pleasant. With such an attitude we have no doubts about returning. We don't feel that we are budget fodder or a statistic, we feel worthy. That's service!

✔ The difficulty is that what one customer service department considers good service is nowhere near the quality of another. But the fact is that under emerging customer demands, they will not survive. In reality, good service costs less, firstly because the biggest value comes from the individual's enthusiasm, and secondly because people do not generally mind paying extra for the pleasure of receiving good service.

✦ This is what was intended by giving a tip, a tradition originating in the eighteenth century at country inns, when the carriage driver or horseman would toss a coin to the stable boy. This advance payment for service was to ensure that everything would be cleaned and ready for the following day, with the horse fed and watered. The incentive encouraged performance and the word 'tip' became colloquial slang for the practice: To Insure Performance. In more recent times the tip has become a *right to receive* which people pay out of customary politeness, more than anything else. Indeed the tip is now added to the bill as a service charge in many establishments, irrespective of the quality of service.

✦ Unconditional service means to do what you do regardless of whether you receive a tip, payment, praise or recognition. Perhaps because of its heritage, our culture is predominantly inclined towards the need to be right and superior, rather than towards providing good service, which is considered subservient. That is why the customer is reticent about complaining, because it requires confrontation with the person serving who, inherently resenting criticism, feels the need to put things right according to the way they see things. The person considered difficult is the person who complains, after all, what do they expect?

❧ A further impediment is the demand by many businesses for its customers to provide feedback. Although intended for future analysis, the compilation of results often takes precedent over providing immediate action in respect of a customer's concern. An individual can seldom resolve a difficulty because they have not been empowered to do so. The machinery of procedure has to take over in order to ascertain blame accordingly.

❧ Developing long-term relationships is not about scoring points or doing favours for others in order to get them on our side. It is not about building a bond based on regular custom. It is about wanting to build success by helping others become successful. It is about helping people help themselves so that they are able to stand on their own two feet and help others in the same way because of our example. It is about using integrity and understanding, rather than relying on legal documents and contracts To Insure Performance.

❧ Such a shift in thinking about how we deal with others requires sowing certain actions on our own behalf. For how can we expect to reap strong relationships with others unless we first correct the way we grow them.

Daily Service

There was once a man who everyone in the village disliked because, although rich, he was miserly.

'You must be very jealous of me to dislike me so much,' he

told them. 'But when I die, I won't take anything with me. I will leave everything to charity, to be used for the sake of others. Then all of you will be happy.'

But the people did not believe him and mocked him. 'What's the matter with you all?' said the rich man. 'I'm not one of the immortals you know, I will die and then all my wealth will go to charities. Why don't you believe me and wait a few years.'

Resenting the fact that no-one would take him at his word he went for a walk. After a short time a downpour of rain started and the rich man had to take shelter quickly under a big tree. At the other side of this tree was a pig and a cow who were in conversation.

'Why is it that everybody appreciates you all the time, and not me?' asked the pig of the cow. 'When I die I provide them with lots of things - bacon, ham and sausage. People even use my bristles, ears and hide. Yet you only provide them with milk.'

'Ah, but you see, I give my milk daily,' answered the cow. 'Everyone can see that I am generous with what I have, whereas you do not give anything to anyone while you're alive. You give only after you are dead. People don't believe in the future, they believe in the present. Those who say they'll give in the future are never appreciated. And until they realise why they are not, they continue to feel resentment. It's quite simple, if you give while you're alive, people will appreciate you.'

'By the beard of my ancestors,' said the rich man to himself, and from that moment he changed.

✦ Self-Reliance is an attribute coveted since ancient times. Being an individual and standing strong is a favoured theme in our culture, and we achieve this state because others helped us to become self-reliant through the lessons and blessing their lives bestowed on us. Whatever we have of any true worth, is because others have served us and we have served them. Being a parent is a worthwhile enterprise, even if it appears thankless.

✤ However scarce is the daily support, thoughtfulness, discipline and teaching we received from others throughout our lives, they have indeed helped to build the sum total of our experience to date. And it is our experience that remains unique to us. Whenever we hold back that which we have gained through the flowing interaction with others we are effectively hoarding.

✤ The root meaning of affluence means 'to flow to.' Conversely, hoarding means to keep contained. Money is a form of energy, a currency that needs to flow and, like blood, it must flow or it begins to cause serious damage. It flows most effectively when the life energy we exchange for it is in the form of service to others. Every relationship is one of give and take, but it is the intention behind it that is important. Whether it is money, the most recognised measure for service, or compassion, love and friendship, the rewards depend on how unconditionally it is given. Whenever something is given conditionally, the person receiving it subconsciously registers this and the strength of a relationship is affected accordingly.

✤ Because the movement of everything in our external world is done for some consideration or other, it is important for us to choose who we want to do things for, what we want to do things for, and why we want to do the things we do. If we do not address these questions then the growth of resentment within us is inevitable.

✸ That is why most people, when faced by a resentful person, either get resentful themselves or try to lower the other person's resentment through appeasement. Both responses are wrong and certainly not conducive to reaping strong relationships. The key is to discover why we allow the resentment of another to affect us, and why we may feel resentment for another. For in doing so, we can become free of it.

✸ The rich man was operating under the misguided belief that in promising others something in the future, he could receive their friendship now. But this is the 'someday I will' syndrome, which is strong in word but always non-existent in deed. Building relationships requires current and consistent actions. Writing a letter to someone because we want to; making a phone call or visit because we want to; and giving, selling or serving because we want to, is the only nurturing that is worthwhile.

✸ Whatever we do comes back to us. If it does not come back from one side, it will come back from another. Suppose, for example, we hurt the feelings of someone junior to ourselves by speaking rudely. Because we consider them subordinate, we think we are quite safe and no harm will come of it. But subconsciously our mind is affected by the insult impressed upon it. We carry that impression with us to whomever we meet, where it brings out the same insulting tendency of the person with whom we come into contact. The element attracts the same element, our coldness attracts their unkindness. We may indeed meet and deal with people who cannot insult us because their situation makes it impossible, but when we meet someone who can do so, the experience will be different.

✔ The manner in which we treat the person behind the desk should be in no way different to the manner in which we treat the person in front of the desk. The view that we are all important customers and valuable suppliers to each other, must be the norm if we are to adopt the emerging values of respect for people and customer care. Allowing them to be simply statements of intent, produced by change initiatives to support erstwhile missions, is surely the height of insensitive arrogance.

✔ Whatever fortunes we are capable of making will most assuredly come from chasing our passion, not our pension. To be motivated to give better performance and service than we are ever paid for will ensure that our commitment and dedication will always be sought after. Knowing that our missions and goals can only be fulfilled through our uncompromising service to others means that we can pursue what we are passionate about, rather than the money.

✔ Many young people commence their careers by trying to get the highest paying job possible, regardless of the industry, opportunity, service or product they have to provide. But when we chase money and success in this way we will always be its slave, waiting for the next deal. Alternatively, by doing only that which we feel passionate about, which we love doing and where we are prepared to deliver more than we promise, then the money will chase us because we will always be in demand.

⌖ The four fingers of commitment, passion, co-operation and dedication are inevitable clasped together into a fist of success by the thumb of service.

Mistaken Identities

Merchant Wang was proud of his adopted son, Tu To. Indeed, he was proud of all of his five other children by birth, but Tu To had done so well. Since finding him wandering on the streets of Han Tan, when he could hardly talk, he had become so helpful and supportive.

'You could do better to learn from Tu To's example,' he lectured his children. 'Consider how he learns the trade so vigorously, the trade I might add that feeds and clothes us all.'

His second son raised his eyes and looked at his father, saying, 'Forgive me sir, but perhaps it is because you treat him more like a customer, and us more like employees.'

Merchant Wang's breath was taken away as the truth of his son's words hit him with such unexpected force. After some moments, he looked at all of his children before him and then addressed his second son, 'Thank you for that, my son, for it is true that a man never believes that he has occupied a certain low level of understanding until a profound truth helps him to rise above it and see the difference for himself. I admit my mistake. I have wrongly been more your employer than your father and have chosen to lecture, instead of listen. From this moment I will try very hard to be a father. But I will need your guidance as old habits stick to an old dog like the fleas it becomes accustomed to.'

'You are both a good man and father already,' replied his son. 'For your actions have always taught us that a man who is good does not go around contriving to be good. It takes compassion to support less fortunate children as your own; it takes courage to admit mistakes; it takes wisdom to want to improve; and it takes love to change for our sake. Together we are all stronger, for a family is greater than the sum of the parts.'

☘ As individuals each of us are prone to misunderstandings, assumptions, hearing half a story and perceiving falsely what we see. All are seemingly the key factors which cause rifts, disputes and breakdown in communications. Often, wanting the best for those around us, we lecture more than listen, certain that the solution we are providing from our own experience is the best. To make mistakes, however, is healthy, for the person who never makes mistakes can never achieve anything worthwhile. In reality it is not the mistakes we make that are responsible for tense human relations, it is the lack of courage in admitting them.

彳 The mistakes that we make in the misguided belief that we will get ahead are by the far the hardest to admit. The mistake of stealing credit from others will always rebound; the mistake of slandering others through thoughtless gossip destroys friendships, marriages and careers; the mistake of rumour spreading, which is as hard to un-spread as butter off bread; and the mistake of too much pride has toppled individuals and empires more frequently than any other mistake since civilisation began.

彳 All of us have experienced regret at things that we have said, and not just those in the heat of the moment. Feeling hurt we have allowed our tongue to cause damage, little realising at the time that the greatest damage is done to ourselves.

彳 Misunderstanding, misconceptions and confusion come directly from our compulsion to react to others. The degree to which we react relates to the degree that we make ourselves see and hear what we believe we want to see and hear. When we allow ourselves to react to another, we are mistakenly identifying that person as a threat, to what we believe are our deep rooted values, even though we may not be consciously aware of what those values are. Ask another, when they least expect it, what they stand for, and the majority will be unable to answer directly.

彳 Asking ourselves is difficult enough. Yet it is our protection of these 'beliefs and values' that causes us to react. The key is to build the habit of standing aside from ourselves, while watching our reactions. By not resisting, condemning, or seeking to change our reaction, we can quietly watch it and let it go. In this way, we do not build internal barriers to listening to another and, through listening, there is less chance of mistaking someone's identity.

✝ It is worth asking ourselves if our tendency is to treat our own family as family, or whether we prefer to lecture, or listen, to the people we work with. It is certainly worth asking whether our tendency is to react to others because they are family, or because they are not family. Do we react because they are employees, employers, customers, clients, competitors, friends or strangers or because they are not? Often we give our family and work colleagues less leeway, because we know them, while adopting a more convivial attitude towards people that we don't know because they prove interesting, are well-known, or carry a title.

✝ Nothing can be more de-motivating than the parent, or employer, who instead of being proud of their child's or employee's performance, dilutes it. Dilution can occur simply from not listening properly, or looking for external reasons for the accomplishment, such as, 'Of course you were lucky to have found that opportunity'; 'But you had help from them of course'; 'Wasn't it Mr Smith's idea?' and 'Well you must get it from me.'

✝ All these well-meaning admonitions are designed to keep the child or employee in their place, so that they do not get big-headed. The fact is that these admonitions only succeed in putting others down and smothering ideas before they even have time to breathe. Such seeds only reap future low self-esteem at best, or even worse, resentment, antagonism and duplication of beliefs.

✦ A helping hand, or kind word sown, can never be underestimated for what it can reap. Merchant Wang's action in adopting Tu To is similar to another story. A poor Scottish crofter upon hearing the plaintiff cries for help from a young boy, rescued him from a bog just in time. The boy's father, a nobleman, offered to educate the crofter's own son in appreciation. In time the Scotsman's son graduated from St Mary's Hospital Medical School, London. He later became Sir Alexander Fleming, the noted discoverer of penicillin. Years later, the nobleman's own son was stricken with pneumonia and would have died were it not for the use of penicillin. The nobleman was Lord Randolph Churchill and his son was Winston Churchill, one of the twentieth century's greatest leaders.

✦ None of us can ever begin to imagine how holding out a helping hand towards another can either directly or indirectly affect the destiny of Mankind. Conversely, we can never imagine what we are taking away from someone because of either a thoughtless word or through lack of praise. It is worth remembering that every bad habit will lead us away from what we want; and from what we are capable of helping others achieve.

✝ Too many of us spend more time criticising ourselves and others than we do praising, and more time remembering what others did wrong instead of what they did right. We must consistently look for the good in others, refusing to react to that which we consider bad.

✝ No-one has the right to mar another person's life, yet many who have spent their lives doing good, are remembered for the one human indiscretion that others insisted must mar it. None of us have the right to cast stones; yet all of us have the occasional habit of picking them up. It is the very act of picking them up that is more the cause of the breakdown in our relations with others than the actual throwing.

✝ In wanting others to accept our foibles and forgive our errors, we must accept the foibles of others and forgive their humanness. In doing so, we are able to let go of our prejudices and compulsions to react, and instead respond courageously by doing or saying what is needed to strengthen a relationship, rather than weaken it. And how must we respond when we are uncertain what to give? It can simply be a kind thought extended to another in silence, for the energy of such a thought is infinitely more strengthening to both parties than the debilitating resentful thought that is too often sent out.

Choosing and Sustaining Relations

'During one particularly difficult winter a certain man thought about how he could reduce his expenses,' began the storyteller to

the listening crowd. 'And he came up with what he thought was a bright idea. He decided to give his hard-working mule a little less grain and hay. This he did and the mule seemed quite content. So, a few days later, he gave it a little less and it still appeared to be happy.

'This continued until the man was giving the animal less than half its normal ration. The mule moved more slowly and was quieter, but the man still thought it was healthy and happy. Then, one morning, much to his surprise, he entered his barn and discovered that his mule had died in the night. This man then wept and cried aloud saying, "My trusty mule is dead and just when he was getting used to not eating."'

The crowd that now surrounded the storyteller roared with laughter. 'What did the fool expect!' shouted someone.

'Exactly so!' said the storyteller. 'To expect the continued support of such a loyal companion, without any sustenance, is foolish. Yet that is how Man himself often behaves towards loyal friends, measuring the strength of their relationships through the lack of complaint they receive.'

'But Man is not an ass,' shouted another bystander, accentuating the last word to another roar of laughter from the crowd. 'He does not have to suffer in silence. When he is hungry everybody knows about it. He is like a bear with a sore head!'

'But when he is hungry for something that really matters to him he is as silent as the night,' said the storyteller. 'People go to bed at night starving for affection, praise and love, more than they ever do for food. For it is their relationships that upset their stomachs more than lack of food.

'In truth, we must never compromise the important relationships in our lives by reducing the level of sustenance *every relationship must have to be strong. We must never take the silence of another as agreement to how well we think we are treating them. Indeed, we must never take any of our relationships for granted, for we might discover that one day the very spark of what was once good has slowly died.'*

✤ True friendship is rare, and a person is considered very fortunate if, during his or her life, there are just a few people he or she can call true friends. But why is such friendship rare? And why do such sayings as 'familiarity breeds contempt' exist? It is important from the outset of any relationship to understand that it must be mutually chosen. It has been said that a person may not be able to choose their family, but they can choose their friends.

✤ If we take the view that the physical plane is a school for souls, then it follows that the spirit will purposely choose a physical host. Doing so helps it to grow and fulfil its ultimate aim of attaining the highest level of consciousness. In this way it will regain the source from whence it came, in a stronger, more evolved form. Its focus is on what will develop it further, as the spirit does not accept that one body is better or worse than another. As such it chooses the most appropriate environment to learn and grow.

✤ Our spirit will choose the parents whose make up, culture, beliefs and environment will be the best influence for growth. The level of friction or harmony which exists is our spirit's perfect incubator, providing the lessons it needs to experience for growth. Taking the premise that we are each here to teach and learn love, we receive our greatest lessons from our family environment, or lack of it. Taking this postulation to its conclusion means that we do, indeed, choose our family. Furthermore, this belief explains why everyone who enters our life, however coincidental, is not by accident. All relationships serve us with a lesson, or perhaps more appropriately, a blessing in disguise.

𝌆 However, no-one disputes that we can choose our relationships. Difficulties arise when we either do not choose, or do not sustain them with sufficient thought. People will always come together according to the influence of the law of attraction. This law attracts like and, paradoxically, attracts opposites. But the opposites that attract must have complementary energies to sustain them.

𝌆 This is because this law is, in turn, ruled by the law of harmony. As in music, it is clear when two notes are in harmony. When they are in disharmony, it is also clear. Two notes may not be in harmony, yet when you add a third it makes a chord. In this way, two people may not harmonise, but a third will create harmony between them. Children, for example, can be the harmonious factor between two people, as can be seen by the many divorces that result when the child leaves home. Similarly, two people may be in harmony together, while a third may create disharmony, resulting in a broken relationship.

✗ To discover whether we can be in tune with another requires us to know what we ourselves are in tune with. This means fully understanding our own likes and dislikes. When we are in tune with our own likes and dislikes, we can more easily develop harmony in our relationships. It is because we do not fully understand the meaning of love that it is important to *like* those people whom we believe we love. In essence this means to give to and to receive from each other.

✗ Familiarity breeds contempt because a relationship is not balanced, with an equal proportion of giving and receiving between two parties. This is because, although the true nature of Man is to give, the predominant conditioned nature of Man is to take. Thus, one person will interpret the friendliness of another in a different manner to that which is intended, and, often unconsciously, take advantage.

✗ Those couples and partners who are able to stay together are those who have come to respect and accept each other because there is giving and receiving in harmonious proportions. That is the basis of all successful marriages, relationships, partnerships and alliances. There must be mutual recognition of what the other needs and brings. Each party sustains the other. When one doesn't, there can follow open discussion and mutual understanding. When this is lacking, then one is inevitably taking the other for granted and the other is allowing them to do so. Both are at fault because they have allowed the discord to take the place of mutual harmony.

✝ How can we be sure that we are choosing a relationship that is right for us? The answer is amazingly simple and relies on three factors. First, each of us has built-in antennae to recognise that which is harmonious to us. Unfortunately, this remains almost totally ignored. Secondly, each of us feels a particular chemistry when interacting with others. Here though, it is important to *interpret* the reactions and responses that we feel *correctly*. And, thirdly, we must consistently work at every relationship. This involves effort but not struggle. When you have to struggle to find a solution in a relationship, then the relationship will eventually fail. Even when it doesn't fail there is always pain, which unfortunately we can become all too accustomed to living with.

✝ What is vital to all relationships is that there should be complementary energies. A person who thrives on conflict may seek out those qualities in another that will fuel them. But this will not be complementary. Similarly, a person who seeks more tranquillity will seek out those qualities that are conducive to sustaining this state. But conflict-needing personalities and tranquil needing ones will not balance each other out either, as they are not mutually compatible energies.

✝ In our concern to ensure that we are in the right relationship, have the right partnership or alliance, we will always tend to seek external advice. Rather be fully aware of what we are in tune with, listen to our own antennae, recognise the right chemistry and then consistently apply effort, we look to a host of other avenues outside of ourselves. These countless external avenues should only be used to confirm our own internal guidance. To decide whether a relationship is right for us because Mercury is in retrograde, for example, makes a mockery of our own capabilities.

Choosing Alliances

⅄ Basing a strategic alliance in business on external advice, when inside you feel differently, also makes a mockery. An effective strategic alliance means that you can gain strength, without getting bigger. In the established global marketplace, no single company can go it alone and be successful. What is important, therefore, is to select the best relationships and alliances for the purpose intended. This involves knowing what makes each party tick, what drives them and what their ultimate goals are. For, unless each party is prepared to assist towards the fulfilment of each other's mission, the alliance will not be sustainable. The best alliances are built when the parties are able to provide complimentary strengths because of their respective experiences and markets. They involve mutual trust, respect and enjoyment, and must share common values.

⅄ Alliances can compromise the fundamental independence of each party and herein lies a difficulty. Management has come to mean total control, and as alliances mean sharing control, managers don't like them. Any alliance is only as strong as its weakest link, and it is individual personalities that make up the relationship links, not legal documents. Unless the people working together understand, like and trust each other, then one will inevitably expect more than the other. Consequently, blame is quickly apportioned when things do not go as planned, with either party being less tolerant than if their own subsidiary was operating in the other's market.

✝ As business alliances are merely a relationship between two energies, the individuals involved must overcome the misconception that control increases success. This need for control is deeply rooted. The very tradition of Western capitalism lies behind it, a tradition that has taught managers the incorrect arithmetic that equates fifty-one percent with one hundred percent control, and forty-nine percent with zero control. With everyone wanting the magical fifty-one percent because it ensures majority control over position, personnel, brand decisions and investment choices, how is it possible to develop the essential mutual ingredients of trust, respect and reciprocity?

✝ Good partnerships, like good marriages, cannot work on the basis of control and ownership. It takes effort, commitment and shared motivation and enthusiasm from both sides if either are to realise the planned benefits. You cannot own a successful partner, any more than you can own a husband or a wife.

✝ Without question, strategic alliances are necessary for business growth, regardless as to whether they involve one-person businesses or conglomerates. But the collaboration must be treated as a personal commitment, because it is people that make partnerships work. Mutual benefit is also vital, which means that both parties will have to recognise from the outset that they will have to give something up.

✔ Because markets change and geographic and corporate cultures are different, it is, of course, important to tie up a legal document. Making sure everything is clearly understood and agreed means that unpleasant and contentious issues can be easily resolved. After that, however, something is wrong with the relationship if the legal document has to be referred to.

✔ The fundamental principle of choosing any alliance must be the same as for all relationships - mutual trust and respect. Whenever we feel that we cannot trust the people we are negotiating with, then despite the rewards that are promised, we must forget the alliance.

The Master of Life

✔ The quality of our lives is reflected in the quality of our relationships. They provide the fundamental environment for our growth, experiences and character, and it is important to choose to reap strong relationships. The degree of pain and heartache we feel is in direct proportion to how weak our relationships are. When those that are important to us are strong, we feel secure; when they are not, we feel insecure.

Every relationship we embark upon requires risk, but the greatest risk is trying to be the person we feel we ought to be, instead of what we are. When we feel the need to play certain roles for others, we are not in tune with what we really want. It is more important to please others through being ourselves, than simply for the sake of feeling we have to please.

✝ Taking the risks required involves wanting to help or serve others unconditionally. Relationships that are based solely on receiving something in return are empty. The best way to serve others is to serve ourselves. This does not mean taking first; it means putting ourselves in order first – for, metaphorically speaking, we cannot complain about the state of our street, if our own house is in a mess. As the best way to learn is often to act, whenever we have the opportunity to help others to help themselves we should willingly do so; for we ultimately help ourselves.

✝ This does not mean being available to those people who interpret our actions in a way as to take advantage of us. But it does mean developing the philosophy of chasing our passion before our pension. It means courageously admitting when we have made a mistake, having the wisdom to improve, and doing so for the sake of our relationships with others. It means choosing our relationships carefully by being in tune with what is right for us as well as for them. And it means sustaining our relationships by providing the support, affection and thoughtfulness that involvement with others requires.

✤ Ultimately, reaping strong relationships with others does not mean putting ourselves last, or others first, as the occasion demands. It means sowing and nurturing what feels right. It means recognising, understanding and accepting that serving another unconditionally does not make us a servant. It makes us a master of life.

Stalking the Heron

Infinite Patience; Immediate Results

*Y*an Kan was worried. *'If I don't catch this bird soon the Emperor will carve me into meat for his dogs,'* he complained to his friend, Cai Tok.

'Yes, thanks to your impulsive outburst about being able to bring him one with no difficulty at all. What demon possessed you to suggest that a mate for his pet heron would bring him great luck?'

'Because I thought it would be a good way for quick advancement,' answered Yan. *'Please help me. Receiving the Emperor's reward for bringing peace to his dynasty will mean high rank to us both and everything that goes with it.'*

It had been some time before when the Emperor had discovered an injured heron in his garden. After it had been nurtured back to health, he had kept it caged, refusing to free it with the argument, *'Herons are omens and now that I have protected it, it in turn will protect me from the ill luck that continually haunts me.'* Much later the bird sickened and began to lose its feathers. When the Emperor exclaimed out loud as to whether there would ever be an end to his misfortunes, Yan Kan, had spoken out with his remedy. So for the past month he had repeatedly tried to catch another heron but to no avail.

'Because of your impatience for a quick result you use methods that won't work,' said Cai Tok. 'This fine creature has an intuitive awareness tuned to approaching danger. You must seek to catch it using the ways of the heron. Observe it. Look for where it rests; for it does not build nests like others, its detachment is its strength. See how it stands, as evenly balanced on one leg as on two, yet as still as stone. Watch how it patiently fishes, immovable while its prey, unaware, swims by. You must be like that.'

After stealthily moving towards the peaceful marsh that his prey frequented, Yan Kan submerged himself in the soggy ground while his friend covered him with the surrounding reed foliage. He soon learned that keeping so still was excruciating and he longed to move. The marsh bed was at least comfortable, he thought, but it was so cold. It was hours later, just when he could hardly bear his imposed prison any longer, that he at last caught sight of the bird. The heron was returning. Knowing he would only have one chance, and would have to be quick, Yan Kan forced all his concentration on what he was to do.

Flying low with legs hanging down, as herons do, the bird did not even touch the ground. Like lightning, a strong hand shot from the harmless-looking reeds and tightly clasped its leg. The surprise attack had been so fast that the startled creature was in a sack before it knew what had befallen it.

The Emperor was delighted and immediately placed the captive with the other. 'There now, my heron, I have a mate for *you. What Emperor would be so generous as that? Between you now, keep my ills at bay!'*

Shivering more from rage than fear, the newly captured heron was surprised to see her forlorn cousin and launched a deluge of questions including, *'But it has been so long, why did you not escape?'*

'That is easy to say,' her cousin replied, *'but another thing to do. I have been impatient to get out for what seems my whole life, but the opportunity has never fallen to hand. Regardless as to how much I squawk and struggle, these bars hold me.'*

'It seems that you have been around humans too long for you have struggled in the wrong way. To be free we simply have to act naturally.'

The next day the Emperor noticed that both birds lay completely still and, as he jolted their cage to stir them, their lifeless bodies remained so.

'What further misfortune is this,' he shouted in horror. *'They must have infected each other with some ill that they independently carried.'*

Opening the cage the Emperor ordered the two dead birds to be removed. Within moments of being laid on the ground both herons immediately took to the sky.

'You see,' said the heron to her cousin, *'patience liberates. I was trapped by patience and now we are free through it. Patience will always bring a quicker result than impatience.'*

'But we might have been buried alive,' the cousin protested.

'Yes, you have been around humans too long,' answered the other.

Having Certainty

🜊 Herons are fortunate in their ability to be patient in fishing for what they want. For his part, Man is unique in placing time constraints on the results that he wants in life and, in doing so, becomes restless, rather than still. It is of course far easier to be patient for something when the outcome of it is certain, because in our certainty, there is less room for anxiety.

🜊 There is a direct correlation between patience and certainty as there is between impatience and doubt. The more impatient you are for something to go the way you want, the more you begin to question whether it will. Say, for example, you begin to question an intuitive idea that you were once certain was right. Your questioning causes you increasingly to doubt it, until you think it is absurd and either ignore it or distort it to fit into your 'perfectly rational' constraints. Although the idea was most certainly right, your rationale, influenced by your impatience to get where you're going, perceives it as wrong, or at least too slow a route to your desired result.

🜊 The key to being patient, therefore, is in having greater certainty of the outcome. But the immediate obstacle for us in accepting such a concept, though, is how can we be certain of an outcome when we can only at best influence an event and time that has not yet happened?

❦ This concept is alien enough to our conditioned thinking, but harnessing the immense power that infinite patience affords requires us to go even further into previously forgotten ways of thinking. Yet in applying the prerequisites of the concept, one begins to recognise, or know again, that it is a *natural* way of thinking; a new unbounded way that produces quicker results, for without doubt patience with another reflects the measure of the patience we have with ourselves. This is the basis of the paradox - only infinite patience produces immediate results.

❦ Before understanding what is involved, stop reading for a moment and, thinking from your heart, rather than your head, reflect on the truth of the following concepts:

1. Harnessing the power of infinite patience will put you at ease.

2. The absolute certainty that what you deeply want for yourself inevitably happens, will free you from your insistence on having it now.

❦ Your thoughts will have re-affirmed what is seemingly common or natural sense. But common sense is rarely common practice. What *is* common practice is allowing the ego's demands, based on fear and impatience, to dominate our thinking. It is the ego that insists on having what it wants now by convincing us how much is missing from our life. If its demands are not satisfied it convinces us how unfair life is to us.

✗ Conversely, if we do satisfy it, it will simply furnish us with another set of demands tomorrow. Freedom from the distracting ego itself is discussed in lesson four, but it is important to understand right now that so long as we allow the ego to dominate our thinking, we will not attain the infinite patience that detachment from outcome requires.

Acknowledging Our Universality

✗ We must seek to cultivate infinite patience through becoming certain about our outcomes, while simultaneously being unconcerned as to when and how. This involves understanding our relationships with everything around us. In the same way that a drop of water taken from the ocean has the same characteristics as its source, so each of us are part of something.

✗ Numerous cultures throughout the ages have referred to this 'something' as an Infinite Universal Spirit. In the West we refer to this Spirit as God. Over the centuries fixed interpretations of God have conditioned us, either wittingly or unwittingly, to believe that this Infinite Spirit is something actually apart from ourselves and indeed jealously sitting in wrathful judgement of us. Enlightenment, or the conscious self-realisation of our oneness with a Universal Spirit, removes this limiting belief.

✗ The New Testament refers to the *Kingdom of Heaven within;* the Holy Koran to *Those who know themselves, know their*

God; the Upanishads, *To know God is to become God* and *by understanding the self, all this Universe is known;* The Tao Teh Ching to *Know that what is, is in everything;* and numerous others appear in every spiritual work; all reminders of our connectedness with a Universal Oneness.

✦ Irrespective of one's faith, or name, term and definition of God, as such a thing is very much a personal choice, acknowledging that you are part of a Universality that is infinite in its possibilities allows you to recognise that what you want cannot be kept from you.

✦ It follows that our ability to trust in this connectedness is proportionate to our ability to *know* that we will receive. This acceptance in turn allows us to remove all demands and time constraints as to how and when we will receive, thus cultivating the virtue of infinite patience. In harmony with other paradoxical truths, the very action of releasing the impeding forces that impatience and attachment unwittingly attract allows the more immediate realisation of what you want.

✦ Take two individuals studying to become proficient in a particular subject. One is desperate to gain recognition of his proficiency and seeks title, badge and award. The other, absolutely certain of the outcome of the dreams that originally motivated him to study, yet unconcerned as to how or when they will be fulfilled, receives recognition ahead of the first. While the first attached his feeling of importance to the award, the other, having let go of such expectations, conscientiously went about his daily business.

✶ Letting go in the knowledge that you will receive is infinitely more powerful than holding on in the hope you may receive, as it places your energy in harmony with the order of the way things work. Admittedly this is a difficult concept to accept, as patiently detaching ourselves from those things which are important to us is in direct conflict with the way we have been taught.

✶ Imagine someone with the following two choices. The first choice is feeling happy only when things turned out just the way they want. The second choice is feeling happy whether things turned out the way they wanted or not. Although the obvious choice is the latter, in reality almost everyone adopts the former. The second choice can only be experienced through the practice of patient detachment.

✶ Consider your involvement with a current situation that holds great importance to you.
- Think about when you want it to reach a fruitful conclusion. Take a moment to observe how you feel.
- Now, in the knowledge that you will continue to go about your business diligently, patiently detach yourself from the outcome.
- Observe how you feel now.
- Say to yourself that because you are absolutely certain that what you want will come to pass; you are completely unconcerned as to how or when it will.
- Observe how you feel now.
- Notice how, if what you were thinking of concerned you, your feelings of frustrations and anxiety diminish.

- Notice also how, if what you were thinking of inspired you, a new certainty smothered rising doubts.

⅄ Although it is good to lose frustrations, doubts and anxiety, your ego begins to feel uncomfortable as its power over you is threatened. Knowing how to squeeze your Achilles heel, it immediately seeks to quell any rebellion by your true self by convincing you that such passive thinking will never gain you what you want. Your impatience is positive, the ego will suggest, as it fuels you to push for what you want and is therefore crucial for your security.

⅄ As these demands increase, your anxiety level increases. The ego does not want you to feel your connectedness with everything, for in allowing that, it removes its main source of power in making you feel unique. The less you feel singled out for what life offers, the harder the ego has to work to convince you that your security is under continual threat. If you become internally driven, rather than externally influenced for your security needs, then the ego is out of a job.

Why Me?

'All my life I have been singled out!' the Emperor complained to Mai-Lee, his favourite concubine. 'The gods have their favourites and I have never been one of them. This Dynasty has been plagued with misfortune, since I became Emperor, despite what I do. What ills did my ancestors perform for me to be treated so?'

'But now that the blue heron is under your protection my lord, a new day will dawn,' consoled Mai-Lee.

'Just so, and in quick time too, or it will bode ill for him,' retorted the Emperor. 'I have told him that as Yan Kan has procured a mate for him so he must use his power to keep away further time-wasting misfortunes.'

The Emperor thought about his five-year rule, in which he had sought to increase his wealth as quickly as possible to avoid future dangers. Didn't his people see that they must all pull together to fill his coffers so that he could protect them? That infernal sage Ti-Ling Tzu had tried to advise him otherwise of course.

'There are three dangers in the world,' Ti-Ling had said. 'To have many privileges but few virtues is the first danger. To be high in rank but low on ability is the second danger. To receive wealth without personally accomplishing much is the third danger. People may gain by loss and may lose by gain.'

What impudence! A leader such as he was beyond such things. Putting the sage to death had been too good for him. Fancy being told that 'the way of rulers is to live frugally so that the citizens will not resent them.' He liked to display his braids of importance. How would everyone respect him otherwise?

Anyway he would be stronger than his predecessors whatever it took, and he would force it to be done in the shortest possible time. He longed for the day when he would be recognised as the most powerful ruler of his dynasty. His former sage had counselled that it would be wise to plan a consolidated growth. But that would take a generation! No, he would do it in one tenth of that time.

'My lord,' cried Mai-Lee waking him from his reverie. *'There is a commotion at the aviary and the keeper begs your attendance!'*

The Emperor had been shocked to see his two herons take to the sky. *'I am being wrongly punished,'* he lamented. *'How can I assure myself of my rightful success when I am besieged by misfortune on all sides? Someone will pay for this unfairness. Where is Yan Kan!?'*

✝ Often when we decide we want something, we want it now, and when we do not get it straight away, we feel that life is unfair, that we have been treated unjustly, even cheated. Sometimes we convince ourselves that it is because others, and even forces beyond us, do not want us to have what we want. In choosing to believe that we have been singled out, we may rationalise that we must do unto others before they do unto us, or, at the very least, get in first before they do, rather than adhere to the Golden Rule of treating others as we would wish to be treated. In taking things personally, we convince ourselves that the acquisition of our desires is at the mercy of the inquisition by others.

✝ Every time we allow ourselves to become impatient, we are devaluing ourselves and failing to trust in the power of our connectedness with everything. In doing so we consider ourselves as separate from a Universal Spirit and assume that if things are not going the way we want, it is because we are being punished for previous misdeeds or are being singled out.

✴ God is not the individual personality with mortal values that Man has created; for a Universal Spirit of unconditional love holds no judgements about one person being more entitled to abundance than another. Since such a Spirit is everywhere in everything, there are no favourites. Punishing you by making all the traffic lights turn to red, or by refusing to grant you a single parking space when you are short of time does not figure in a great design. It is our own confused thoughts that attract the seemingly chaotic events we experience.

✴ To view the realisation of what you want as a favour is to begin the process of *bargaining* with God, which most do more acutely when their needs must. Seeking to strike deals stems from believing that every individual is separate from other living beings. Universal Spirit responds to you when you recognise it for what it is: something of which you are very much a part. In accepting this you are able to attract what you ardently want, and which already exists, to yourself.

✴ Admittedly, this is not immediately digestible. Our daily actions of judging and evaluating others form a continuous stream of affirmations that render any understanding of our connectedness with others impossible. Just because we are physically separate, however, it does not follow that we are metaphysically separate. Metaphorically speaking, each of us have an *extended* interconnected body that has the ability to manifest, through an intricate system of receivers and transmitters contained within our physical body, whatever we choose to attract or emit.

✗ Each of us is like an individualised energy wave sending out and receiving thoughts which co-ordinate or tune-in with matching vibrations. Being impatient, for example, will cause you to emit, and thus attract, a different level of vibration which, although it will match what you unconsciously asked for, is not what you actually wanted.

✗ When you practice infinite patience towards an outcome, you literally transmit an *undistorted* wave of energy for your extended body to receive. Your extended body locates the existence of the objectivity that matches the subjectivity of your transmission, and manifests it for you. The result is quicker because the intention transmitted is infinitely clearer. Our extended body will not recognise our demands as to how and when it should deliver to us; it will only recognise the clarity of why we want to receive. Demanding that God delivers according to a particular timetable and format, reinforces the false idea of God as a disconnected force. There is Infinite Power in the universe and you are connected to it.

✗ The level of consciousness required to manifest objects instantaneously is known as 'siddhi consciousness'. It is a level when the period of pure thought, from transmission to receiving, is instantaneous. Sri Sathya Sai Baba, who millions claim is an Avatar of our age, has attained this level of consciousness. Living in Puttaparthi, Southern India, his manifestations have been witnessed and recorded by the most respected Western and Eastern professional institutions. One can only suppose that as this level requires complete faith in accepting that we are one with God without limitation, this would preclude any abuse of such immense power.

✈ Although each of us holds the potential to attain such a level of consciousness, we have conditioned ourselves within our environment, not to require it. What we are able to accomplish, however, are more immediate results simply through patience.

✈ Experiencing it is by far the best way to see the results that it delivers. Over a seven-day period, make a list of everything that is important for you to achieve, either short-term or long-term. Focus particularly on those elements that, however small, seem to frustrate you - they literally try your patience. During this time become conscious of whenever you feel impatient or frustrated. Each time you feel these emotions remind yourself that you are entirely unconcerned as to when or how the object that is causing your impatience or frustration will come about, or be resolved. Just say to yourself that you are certain that whatever the outcome, it will be in your best interests.

✈ Persevere and you will be astounded at what will happen. Be aware of things that begin to show up in your life which you have not noticed before. Although they may not be quite what you're expecting, the frequency with which they appear will make you more conscious of them. Act on whatever you begin to notice, while trying very hard to release all judgement towards events. Trying to prejudge the result is a sure indication that you are once again becoming attached to the shape of life as it used to be.

✝ The synchronistic happenings you are experiencing are resulting from a heightened consciousness prompted by your patient detachment. At this level you are now consciously making contact with the universal source of energy that was previously below your conscious level. Remember to act on the things that are now coming to you, as this signals to the universe that you are ready to receive. Whether or how you thank your connectedness to the Universal Spirit for sending you the people and events to fulfil the right outcome for you is, of course, a matter of individual choice.

The Instruction of Obstruction

'So his obsession for not letting go of anything finally caught up with him,' commented Yan Kan to himself, on hearing news that the Emperor had met with an untimely end.

It had been several years now since Yan Kan had fortuitously escaped the Emperor's wrath. It had been his experience of stalking the heron that had led him to see things in a different light. When water accumulates, it breeds predatory fish. And when rites and duties become decorations, they breed artificial and hypocritical people. The title and rank that the Emperor had quickly invented and thrown to him that day, and which he had so obsequiously caught, were now empty and meaningless to him.

He had decided that moment to apply his new-found virtue of patience to more meaningful pursuits and departed the Court. He would no more attach such importance to such false things. And he would no more suggest solutions that sought reward by pandering to the whims of another in authority. Any leader who demanded, needed or revelled in such bolstering was an insecure leader. How strange it is that when rulers have obsessions, their subjects do a lot of posturing; when a ruler is crafty, their subjects are devious; and when a ruler is demanding, their subjects are contentious. Any ruler who blamed ill luck for the state of his kingdom and sought to determine outcomes by using his strength to hold on to something weaker, was bound to fall sooner or later.

Yan Kan felt no surprise that the Emperor had lost his life through his rigid attachment to his policy for growth and recognition. His wise friend Cai Tok had been right: 'When political leaders ruin their countries and wreck their lands, themselves to die at others' hands, it is always because of their impatient desires.'

Since becoming a merchant, Yan Kan had determined to himself that he would follow the sage-like philosophy he now knew to be true: 'To be able to use the power of other people, it is necessary to win people's hearts. To be able to win people's hearts, it is necessary to have self-mastery. To be capable of self-mastery, it is necessary to have patience.'

Yan Kan resolved to apply patience in everything, particularly when he encountered the obstacles which he had discovered were as much a part of business as they were of life.

'The ancients were certainly wise in creating writing symbols that contained the meanings of both crisis and opportunity. I

will see every obstacle as a further reminder to be infinitely patient and unattached to any particular schedule. For in such flexibility lies the power to cultivate the hidden pearl of opportunity from the grit of adversity.'

ϒ To have the virtue of patience, it is important to acknowledge obstacles as opportunities to strengthen you, not as indications of failure. In attempting to patiently let go of an outcome, there will be a tendency to view obstacles that begin to appear as evidence that what you are embarking upon is not working. The ego will always use such obstacles as proof to deny the existence of your connectedness to a universal energy. In doing so it attempts to regain its influence over you, which your new actions of patience and detachment are causing it to lose.

ϒ Detaching yourself from an outcome does not mean giving up on it. Determination and persistence are valuable ingredients in both testing your resolve and surmounting life's inevitable obstacles. The message of this lesson must not be misinterpreted as the opportunity to just sit back and do nothing; thinking that everything will be taken care of. It is to continue to ensure that you go about your daily routines, relative to what you are working towards; while being unconcerned as to the outcome, certain that it will be right for you in some form.

ϒ The art of receiving immediate results for yourself through infinite patience lies in occupying a higher state of awareness; rather than allowing yourself to feel that you are being pushed around by whims that are out of your control. Consider the difficulties that have caused you to re-evaluate your life in order to surmount them. Such reflection will confirm that each one was both timely and appropriate, although it might not have seemed so at the time.

Your reflection will also reveal to you that having more patience would have surmounted the difficulty with less pain than your impatience gave you. However, when you are impatient to get out of something or into something for that matter, you are more liable to compromise yourself. The fact is that every obstacle you encounter offers the opportunity to propel you to this higher state of awareness. It provides a test for your certainty of attaining what you have resolved to attain. There is no timetable when you have infinite patience and there can be no failure when you have detached yourself from how the desired result will come about.

> Patience builds serenity.
> Great people are serene, free from longing;
> They are composed, free from worry.
> Being calm and joyous, without pride,
> One attains harmony.
> Harmony is the essence of Oneness
> From which immediate results derive.

Shooting the Monkey

Freedom from the Distracting Ego

*I*nvited to a grand reception Chang did not dress for the occasion. Arriving in his everyday clothes he was treated with disrespect and contempt. No-one paid him any attention and the servants did their utmost to ignore him, not even serving him dinner. Slipping out unnoticed, Chang went home and changed into the finest silk tunic, belt and robes adorned with breath-taking jewellery, a magnificent turban and an expensive overcoat.

Returning to the banquet he was received with open arms. Although all harboured their individual hidden agenda and a little envy, the hosts were delighted to see such a man of obvious importance and asked him to sit with them at the highest table, offering him a plate filled with the choicest delicacies. Then, much to the bewilderment of the hosts and everyone present, Chang removed his coat and turban, placed them before the plate and said: 'Eat, my master, eat.'

'What are you doing?' one of the astonished hosts enquired.

'It is my apparel that you are honouring, not me,' replied Chang.

❯ That conscious, thinking part of each of us that seeks security to an external reality, whether through what we do, who we are, how we appear, or what we have, is fundamentally our ego. Our ego is not a fact, it is an idea; an idea that has pervaded our entire thinking, establishing limitations and boundaries in our beliefs about ourselves. It is an idea that has resulted from perceiving ourselves as a separate individual entity that requires utmost security and protection because it is superior, different or apart from others.

❯ Man has two 'selfs' – a lower, being our ego; and a higher being our *true* Self. The lower is constantly preoccupied with the virtues of its attributes; wanting others to obey moral precepts only as *it* expounds them. Obsessed with presenting itself in ways that gain the good opinion of others, it continually directs a person to pretensions so that people will compliment and praise it. But while praising others in their presence, its tendency is to do the opposite in their absence.

❯ The ego-self is the creature born of our own thinking and doing. Forming the sum total of all our memories, habits, opinions and thought-patterns, it is a helpful frame of reference and can be a useful tool. But although its services are handy, we have allowed it to become our master, rather than our servant, by failing to recognise that its view of how things should be for us only restricts and frustrates us. Considered and often defined as a separate entity, or reality in its own right, it is actually a reflection, albeit extremely limited and distorted, of our higher-self.

✔ Our goal must be to allow one to shine through the other, by fulfilling ourselves and learning greater intimacy with our higher-self. In this way, we transcend our ego and escape its bondage, allowing it to be used freely and compassionately with wisdom. When we do not, and continue to be unaware of our ego's false protection, we are only successful in becoming our own worst enemy.

With everyone's attention on him, Chang began to share a story about a wise old sage whom people visited from near and far to seek advice on personal problems.

One day a man awkwardly carrying a large sign struggled up to where the sage lived. His sign read:

Here Is a Very Important Person
Who Always Knows What He Is Doing

'The problem I need you to solve,' said the visitor to the sage, 'is how to lighten the terrible weight and irritation that carrying this sign causes me. Please show me how I can do so more comfortably.'

'There is no way, other than the way you currently use,' replied the sage. 'But you can let go of it altogether, although you must have the courage to do so. Yet, in so doing you will gain more.'

Not hearing the words of advice he had travelled so far for, the man snapped with hostility, 'But you don't understand, this sign has served me well for many years by attracting money, honour and friends. You cannot begin to imagine how many people believe it simply because they see it. I do not want to think about life without it, as I have become so used to it. I merely want to learn how to keep the sign, while making it more comfortable. It is clear to me, oh wise one,' continued the man sarcastically, 'that you are not as clever as you think you are.' Bidding the sage a cursory good day, he stumbled away with his heavy load.

Concluding his tale, Chang said to those present, 'It is a strange thing that a person is satisfied with so little in himself, but demands so much in others. The emptiest man is the man who is full of himself, for as we all know,' he chuckled, 'the fellow who thinks he is full of knowledge is especially annoying to those of us who are.'

✦ True success in life begins with the subordination of the ego. This means first acknowledging the power that we have allowed our ego to have over us, by recognising its insistent and insatiable demands. Then we must let go of our need to impress others. Such needs generate the insecurities that cause us to put all our efforts into obtaining something perceived as really important. It may be a comment that you feel threatens your skill, position or status. It may be the need to have a better car, house, clothes or holiday as a measure of your success in front of other people. Acting as a comfort blanket, our ego influences our decisions with misguided thoughts of security. Thoughts, which appear to be in our best interests in the short term, actually cause us to work against ourselves in the long term.

✦ The difficulty is that no matter how much we feed the ego, it delivers a new list of demands immediately after its previous ones are satisfied. Whatever you give it will never be enough, for it operates in the belief that having more means better security, recognition and importance. And, whenever your ego feels your needs are not being met, it demands that you complain about why you are not getting what you should.

✸ The ego wants what it wants immediately, although it does not dwell in the present. Its power is in the past and future, over what should have been, or what ought to happen. Although when satisfied it demands more, when it is unsatisfied it convinces you of how unfair life is and what an awful place the world is. Insecurities increase in direct proportion to the ego's greater control over your life. Thus we look more and more outside of ourselves to fill the emptiness that increasingly grows inside.

✸ Of course it is hard to be aware that our ego is detrimental to us when it has successfully convinced us that it is protecting us. But when we do become aware of it, and are able to recognise its false demands, it can then be used as an ally rather than a foe. Our ability to regain mastery over our ego requires awareness and understanding of four paradoxical keys. These are: Distraction Attraction; Simplified Complexity; Separated Oneness; and Fearful Love.

Distraction Attraction

'Has Your Majesty never observed the bounding monkeys?' *answered Chang to the King of Wei. 'If they can reach the tall*

cedars, or camphor trees, they will swing and sway from their limbs, frolicking and lording it in their midst, so that even the famous archers Yi or P'eng Meng could not take accurate aim at them. But when they are attracted to what they suppose are delicacies and find themselves among the prickly mulberries, brambles, hawthorns, or spiny citrons, way below their loftier arena, they must move with caution, glancing from side to side, quivering and shaking with fear.

'It is not that their bones and sinews have become suddenly stiff and lost their suppleness. It is simply that the monkeys find themselves in a difficult and disadvantageous position, one where they cannot exercise their abilities to the full. And so it is when Man becomes full of himself. His attraction to what is seemingly of benefit and greater security to him actually distracts him from expressing himself in his full light.'

'I like that tale,' said the King of Wei, 'but knowing you as I do, I have no doubt that the monkey is merely a metaphor for Man's own mischievous self. Our fall from our true identity causes us to improvise and clutch at a false identity with the same desperation as someone falling continuously into the abyss.'

'Exactly so!' said Chang gleefully. 'In the absence of the true knowledge of who we really are, our adopted self must keep alive its fictional existence with convincing, albeit empty, chattering.'

'Chattering which is taken to heart rather than ignored,' said the King. 'Incessant and sweet chattering thoughts that, while sometimes a nuisance, sweetly persuade, convince, cajole, even scare us into believing that if we want protection, security and peace of mind, there is no other self worth listening to.'

*'And if such a self was indeed a monkey, how would you, as
a sagely King, deal with it?' enquired Chang.*

*'Why I would ensure that both Yi and P'eng Meng practised
harder, until they were successful,' his monarch replied with
amusement.*

*'And how so for your own self, is it also a case of shooting
the monkey?' asked Chang.*

*'Again, I would employ and develop those decisive archer
parts of my own being to unmask myself.'*

*'Well said, my King, for only by such action will you rid
yourself of a fictional power that ultimately renders you
powerless.'*

☩ Both modern psychology and education is based on the
idea that, unless a person has a strong ego, he or she cannot
succeed in life where there is so much competition. The
feeding of the ego, therefore, begins almost immediately,
through teaching people, either consciously or unwittingly,
not to be the best they can be, but to be better than others.
Success is defined by what a person has achieved in
comparison to others, rather than in relation to what they
themselves are capable of, but have not yet achieved.

☩ Our whole society is geared to develop the assertive,
competitive elements within us, rather than the resolute, co-
operative elements. A person will refer to his tutelage of a
new recruit, for example, by saying, 'I taught him everything
he knows.' In so doing he is maintaining his seniority and
position over the pupil. To say 'I taught him everything I

know, and look - he has surpassed me with his progress,' is too much of a threat to even consider.

❦ The actor, who receives a lesser billing than his up-and-coming younger protégé, will view them as a Brutus. A recently promoted director will not be comfortable until his appointment is formally announced and he has the office, car, house, and expense account that reflect his new position. The importance of these endorsements will occupy a person's thinking, distracting them from their new responsibilities. After all, if it is in title only, what will everyone think?

❦ Although elements of the ego are useful as a tool, when the very need to succeed becomes the very means and end of what we do we suffer a kind of implosion. The mushrooming cover that we exude becomes unstable for the stalk that supports it, so that when, not if, we continue to subject ourselves to those notions and whims we deem so important, our world inevitably comes tumbling down.

❦ Doing what is important, above what is urgent is obviously the key, but this is not possible without first acknowledging what is important in our life. It is because of the meaningless void in our life that our ego attaches itself to what is considered vital for its survival. Not knowing what is important, our tendency is to drop down to the depths of life's numerous distractions, all eager to feed our hungry ego. Receiving praise for work done is a distraction that we allow to take precedent over the work itself. Praise, recognition and being part of accepted society, particularly its élite, are considered more important than the work that we do to express ourselves; so that only reward becomes our motivation.

✝ Reward is certainly a positive motivation in its rightful place, but not when it becomes the sole purpose for what we do. The monkey trained to climb palm trees to retrieve coconuts, does so simply for the reward and praise it receives. In a short time the monkey gets bored with what it has to do, however, and begins to refuse. Yet it will not give up its reward as this has become a right. But what of Man?

✝ Man's lower self also soon wearies of having to do things that do not interest it, yet similarly, it will not give up its reward. Indeed the ego demands the reward by convincing Man that, because of his position and what he does, receiving reward is his right. When the reward is no longer forthcoming, for whatever reason, a person will consider its removal as an infringement of personal rights.

✝ Often the ego is only interested in reaping, not sowing. Take the example of two individuals both operating from different perspectives. The first person, a graduate, expects greater rewards than another person who has practical experience but no qualifications. Similarly, the latter person considers his reward should be greater. The former's ego rejects the fact that he has never managed others before, or cannot manage himself; while the latter's ego rejects the fact that he lacks understanding of specific managerial skills. Both, however, want the reward that qualification *and* experience achieve; one because his tutor advised him that he should expect nothing less than management status, the other because he has been there longer.

✙ It is the ego that is in control, seeking the best reward for the least input, rather than seeking reward for being the best of their ability, in due course. Further attractions then follow sequentially, as each is obtained: type of car; size of work-area; position and size of desk; size of expense account; location of office; and so on. Circumstance is irrelevant when external attractions are deemed vitally important to security.

✙ Our ego causes us to focus in on what we can have, rather than be. It wants you to have, without having to do and to do without having to be. It can devise whatever fictional being, in the form of title or name, it considers is necessary for your protection. Answering the question of what you will *buy*, if you won a million pounds, is easier than answering the question of what you would *be*. There is of course nothing wrong with ambition, indeed, we must be ambitious to survive, grow and fulfil our potential. But where the human desire to succeed is very positive, a preoccupation with personal ambition that keeps us constantly wound up and measures success in comparison to others is not.

✙ With the focus of our attention meeting the demands of our ego, we insidiously revolve our lives around trivia. Metaphorically attracted by what the monkey is wearing, and how it performs, we are distracted from hearing the music that the organ-grinder plays for us. This is why so many of us go to our graves with the symphony of our true selves remaining un-played. Similarly, attracted by the infinite number of toys that we must have to add credence to what we do and what we are, we are consistently distracted from that which we should really occupy ourselves with.

🗡 History, however, records that great men and women have lived by the philosophy: 'Whatever anyone thinks of me, is really none of my business.' King Alfred is remembered for ignoring all trivia by burning the cakes. Lord Nelson is remembered for ignoring all trivia by turning a blind eye. Trivia is not detail, it is the whims, notions, suggestions and interferences that both your own ego and those of others insist you pay attention to.

🗡 Next time you do something for another, take time to consider why you are doing it; next time you buy something, consider why; next time you seek the credit for something, notice how you feel when you don't get it – threatened, cheated, left out? If you have an expense account do you treat it as if it were your own money? If someone books you in economy, rather than business class, do you feel your position or status is threatened? Is what you have and receive in relation to what you do, more important to what you do and give in relation to what you are?

🗡 Do you think that great people would concern themselves about such things? Are you concerned about what people think of you? Are you allowing your ego to distract you from being great, by being attracted to what society or media deems is great to have? As one sage said, 'The lower-self is like a flame both in its display of beauty and in its hidden potential for destruction; though its colour is attractive, it burns.'

Subordination of the ego requires an awareness of the toys and other attractions that distract us from being our true-self, and which we use to decorate our fictional self; attractions that our ego causes us to believe are essential for our protection. This level of awareness can only be developed through involvement with something that is greater than ourselves. Whenever we seek to make a difference in the lives of others through what we do, we begin to control our ego. Those who are controlled by their lower-self must serve it; those who control the lower-self, serve others. To serve others in such a way that your own success is built on helping the success of others, requires understanding of the second key.

Separation towards Oneness

Saddened that his only son had run away, a father searched without success. After a few years he chose to settle in a town and, being exceedingly wealthy, he built a fine mansion.

The son, having impulsively attached himself to some travellers after hearing their stories, had in time forgotten all about his home, unaware of his rightful inheritance by birth. Endlessly wandering through foreign lands, the boy soon fell into the habit of just scratching out a living.

There came a time, however, when the son felt drawn back towards his own country, and one day he wandered unknowingly into his father's town and approached the mansion looking for work. Upon seeing the magnificence of the mansion and the greatness of the owner walking the terrace, however, the destitute young man convinced himself that his labour would not be required. So he began to move on. But his father, never forgetting his beloved son's face for one minute, immediately recognised him amongst the crowd outside the gates. Overjoyed he quickly dispatched his most valued retainers to welcome his son home. Noticing these two well-dressed men hurrying towards him, the son unfortunately mistook their intentions. Fearing that he was about to be blamed for something and imprisoned, he fought them off and ran into the slums for refuge.

After hearing what had happened, the father decided upon a different course of action. Sending two more servants, this time dressed in shabby clothes, he instructed them to find his son and offer him, in conversation, some menial labour on the estate. In this way the son started work within his father's mansion. Each day he engaged in his task of clearing an enormous heap of rotting rubbish, returning to the slums each night. In time, becoming more comfortable with his surroundings, the man quit the slums, accepting the use of a humble estate dwelling house. To get closer to him, the father would dress in work clothes, encouraging the young man in his work, and inviting him to visit the mansion house sometimes.

Working faithfully, his responsibilities increased until in time he became the overseer of the entire estate. But, continuing to feel subservient to his benefactor and unworthy of his generosity, it took more time before the son's diminishing sense of *inferiority allowed him to develop a strong and friendly relationship with his father.*

The time came when the father felt that his death was approaching. Calling together everyone that was involved with the estate, he announced that the poor man that he had taken in years before and now entrusted with the management of the estate, was in fact his own beloved son to whom all his property now belonged. At last the man was enlightened to the truth and was amazed at how his earlier delusions had caused him to believe that he was separate from what had been his rightful inheritance.

⚘ The father represents our true-self and the son our ego-self. The story illustrates how, through choice, we separate ourselves from the whole that makes us one with everything else. Similar to the fall from grace, the eviction from the Garden of Eden, the wandering in foreign lands and the forgetting of our true inheritance, the story symbolises the urge and journey of the human consciousness back towards wholeness. The level of our separateness from all nature as a whole is represented by the extent to which we have wandered into foreign lands, forgotten our birthright and family or connectedness with everything, and live as a destitute, preoccupied with scratching out a living.

⚘ By accepting our delusions of being a separate entity, we limit ourselves to what we consider our status quo should be and become preoccupied with seeking external gains to fulfil our habitual needs. But there comes a time in everyone's life when each one of us feels drawn back to a union with what we really are part of.

✻ Yet before we can rejoin, there is often an enormous heap of rotting rubbish – delusions, hang-ups, phobias and insecurities – to clear away first. That part of us that recognises our connectedness, allows us to move forward only at the rate that is comfortable for our ego, however long it takes. Forcing it will have the opposite effect, as the ego is a part of us and cannot be destroyed. But it can be subjugated and turned into a servant instead of permitting it to remain a master.

✻ The death of the father, and the son's realisation of his true identity, represents the end of the separation between the true-self and the ego-self, and the death of the self-inferiority. The son is no longer deluded by false limitations. Everything on the journey happened when he was good and ready. He would not have anything forced on him, but by developing faith in himself he was able to take on the management of the whole estate. In other words, he was able to take responsibility for becoming his whole self and acknowledge what it involved.

✻ As the ego lies to itself, to the person who identifies with it and to others consistently, then training our ego-self to accept that its separation is a delusion is challenging. Enlightenment initially involves the realisation that you are at one with everything else. But accepting that the Universe is a complete unit, with nothing divided in it, is unacceptable to

the ego. Indeed it shakes the three pillars of separatism: *my,*
mine and *I*, the stalwarts of egoism. Egoism is the belief that
the organism to which *I* am attached is superior to others, so
that *I* measure others by my likes and dislikes, not by their
needs; *I* impudently criticise another for making a slip, while
being guilty of making bigger blunders. Egoism is *I, I, I.*

✦ The real enemy is not the entity ego, which is part of us,
but the function of egoism that thrives on making us separate
and isolated. Egoism is the very glue with which we get stuck
to ourselves. It is not about thinking too much of yourself,
rather it is about thinking too little of other people. It is
about hiding one's misguided sense of inferiority behind the
façade of a superiority complex.

✦ Egoism, therefore, causes us:
* to want to control other people, rather than appreciate
  them;
* to exploit others on a 'what's it in for me basis,' rather
  than seek ways to serve them;
* to be more concerned with competition, rather than direct
  our focus to co-operation;
* to seek win:lose situations, rather than develop win:win
  relationships;
* to cut a good deal for ourselves, rather than want another
  to profit as much as we do;
* to be more concerned in acquiring things, rather than
  giving of ourselves;
* to increase our ownership of goods, rather than being
  willing to share with others;

- and to be more focused on our personal-self, rather than our universal-self.

✔ The truth, however, is that the less self-centred we learn to become, the more we are in tune with others and can enjoy our universal-inheritance. When we can begin to accept that there are other beliefs, we embark on the journey towards realisation that we are not separate entities, but are all one. This great truth of oneness is the ultimate experience because our conscious realisation of it removes the limitations that we have allowed ourselves to have in our lives.

✔ Everything in the universe operates under the same metaphysical laws. But the prime force behind those laws is a Universal Spirit of Infinite Life, Power and Intelligence. Similar to the varying sizes of ocean waves that in their real form are all water, each of us is an individualised spirit which does not differ in essence from this Spirit that we are all part of. It follows that our individualised powers are potentially without limitation, because we are connected to its very source. Indeed, the only limitations we have are the very same ones we set ourselves, by virtue of believing we are separate entities. Comparing ourselves with others, either feeling superior or inferior, therefore, is as absurd as the small wave that compares itself with a large wave.

✔ Hearing sage-like aphorisms of: *'the only things we never lose are the things we give away'*, they affect us because deep-down we know that they are true. Yet our ego does not want us to reflect on such thoughts, as they undermine the belief that we are separate and need to be protected. It immediately replaces them, therefore, with false thoughts such as, *'we deserve more than we have, and anything we give away we will have to do without.'* In doing so it re-establishes its control over us, refocusing our mind as to what we need to maintain our security. 'Giving to get' is an inescapable law of the ego, which always evaluates itself in relation to other egos. It is therefore continually preoccupied with the belief in scarcity that gave rise to it. The ego literally lives by comparisons and equality is beyond its grasp.

✦ Metaphysically each of us is constantly drawing to us the conditions that fit our dominant thoughts. That is why it is so vitally important to keep our minds on what we want, and not on what we *don't* want. Our conditioned difficulty is clearly that, even that which we think we want will not be in our long-term best interests if the desire has originated from egotistical thinking. Whenever we strive to acquire that which we believe protects us, we are actually strengthening the ego and weakening our inheritance.

Personal Labels

✦ From the cutting of the umbilical cord our quest to discover who we are commences. As a child we begin to possess; we think, this toy is *mine,* this mother is *mine.* The reason why all scriptures uniformly advise working to become non-possessive, is that with possessiveness hell starts. Small children jealously and possessively guard their toys, while trying to snatch everything from everyone else. Some children will fiercely cling to a toy, ready to hit and fight if necessary over any infringement of their territory and domination.

✴ Once the idea of *mine* exists you are a competitor with everybody, embarking on a journey of struggle, conflict, violence and aggression. The next step is *me*. Having something to claim generates the beginning of the idea that you are the centre of your possessions. Like the spider in the centre of its web, possessions become your territory, a personal universe that gives rise to the idea of *me* and *mine*.

✴ Labelling yourself '*me*' defines a boundary. This is the beginning of where things go wrong, as you rely on defined ego boundaries to separate yourself from others. From the reflection of *me* within these boundaries arises *I*, the subtlest and most crystallised form of possessiveness. The *I* cannot relax, as it exists through tensions, creating new worries, concerns and fears. But the *I* we create emanates from a false centre. At the real centre, the whole existence is one, just as all the sun's rays emanate from one source of light.

✴ A false centre and identity is manufactured because without boundaries we struggle to compartmentalise who we are, something that society insists that we do. Our tendency when meeting others, for example, is to immediately seek to get a handle on them for what they do, or have done. Unless we can label or compartmentalise them according to our own frame of reference, they make us uncomfortable. We even perceive them as a threat. So, given a name and some idea of who we are by others, we gather the things people say about us and develop a certain image.

✗ Somebody says we are beautiful, another says we are intelligent, another says we are important. But as our inner reality is not available to anybody else except ourselves, the image is going to be false. The ideas that we gather from others may give us personality, but the knowledge we come to know through understanding our true selves gives us individuality, an authenticity that can never be borrowed, unlike personality.

✗ Even though we have been taught for centuries to *'know thyself'*, we never really listen. Too intent on being the person we pretend to be to bother about it, we go on clinging to anything from the outside that may assure us of who we are. The fact is that no-one, other than you, can say who you are.

✗ But how we develop *is* part of a process, a process that involves losing one's self, before we can regain it. The infant without its ego boundaries may be in closer touch with reality than its parents, but it is incapable of surviving without their care. And it is incapable of communicating its wisdom. Ego boundaries have to be hardened before they can be softened, and an identity, however false, must be established before it can be transcended.

✗ Often it is our growing awareness of our own mortality that causes us to seek the path of knowing ourselves. The death of a close friend, or the ending of a particular cycle in our lives, a metaphorical death in itself, is often the catalyst for wanting to understand our own spirituality. Perhaps the best idealist must first be a materialist, as it is easier to give up something you have either first acquired, or experienced.

� Increasingly, people are seeking greater meaning and purpose in their lives. Perhaps, having settled on the shore of what was believed to be the land of fulfilment, we are discovering that it is not as fruitful as we had thought. As if recognising that the sight of one shore must disappear before an alternative can be sighted, people are embarking on their own particular spiritual journey, a voyage that must pass through what is seemingly a sea of emptiness, before their destination is reached.

✲ The Western world is gradually choosing sustainable quality over disposable quantity; businesses are seeking to develop the co-operation essential to serve mutual customers; people are becoming more aware that the key is to think, *we, us* and *ours*, rather than carry labels of *me, my* and *mine*. An increasing wave of consciousness embracing the understanding of our connectedness is recognising the benefits in moving away from egotistical separation.

✲ To recognise the separateness of the ego is the first step; to discern the falsity and absurdity of the movements of egoism is the second; to discourage and refuse it at each step is the third. But it can only be completely subjugated when one begins to perceive, experience and acknowledge that everything is equally connected everywhere. Lasting enlightenment, or spiritual growth, can only be achieved through the persistent exercise of real compassion for creation as a whole, including one's fellow beings.

Simplifying Complexity

An Emperor was travelling the country with his enormous entourage of courtiers and advisors, when he came upon a remote village that he had not visited before. The custom of the countryside was such that people would always offer an Emperor their very best. But the villagers had nothing of value to offer, so they sent their elders to the Emperor to tell him, 'We have something precious to offer you that has been handed down by our ancestors.'

Seeing nothing in their hands, the Emperor asked, 'What is it?'

The spokesman for the elders stepped forward and replied, 'In the wintertime, if you sit in the sunshine you will feel very comfortable.'

Bemused by their answer the Emperor began to laugh, as did the whole entourage. 'Everyone knows that, it is no secret,' he said, 'but I accept your simple yet "precious" gift.'

Returning home, the Emperor reflected on the words of the village elders. 'Life is simple yet man makes it complex,' he thought. 'As an Emperor I can have anything I want, yet the more I have, the more complicated my life becomes. My life is more a reflection of what others expect an Emperor to be, rather than how I truly am. Their reflection has become my reality. I do what I do because I am expected to, because I am able to, yet it seems that there is little time to just live.'

⸸ The ego will cling fiercely to whatever false and complex structure it deems essential for our security. Indeed, it welcomes complexity above anything else, as it considers that greater complexity means more challenging stimulation. Thus, there is a tendency within our personal and professional lives to complicate rather than simplify things. Despite the fact that waste thrives on complexity, most businesses engage in it, generating prodigious amounts of needless, unproductive and expensive activity. The greater the sense of importance attached to being involved with what is complex, the greater the activity and the less the productivity.

⸸ In a material-focused world, where success means having more, activity is mistaken for productivity. Consequently, activities are focused on that which brings about greater importance and complexity, because they will bring the rewards and recognition that are seen to be necessary for a person's protection. In reality, because the ego is only concerned with illusory protection, nothing lasts, and the more a person feels they have to protect, the more insecure they feel.

Sage, Yang-Chu, once said to his Emperor, 'People will always be active in seeking satisfaction in good food, fine clothes, lively music and sexual pleasure. Many will in time realise that meeting their material needs does not create the happiness hoped for. So society becomes active in setting up reward systems that go beyond material goods.'

'You refer to such things as titles, social recognition, status and political, bureaucratic and organisational power,' said the Emperor, 'all wrapped up in a package called self-fulfilment.'

'Exactly so,' said Yang-Chu. 'Attracted by such prizes and goaded on by social pressure, people spend their lives actively chasing after these goals, feeling that they have achieved something. But the reality is that they have sacrificed a lot in their life because they can no longer productively see, hear, act, feel or think from their hearts. Everything they do is dictated by whether it leads to social gains. In the end, they've spent their lives following the demands of others, never living their own life.'

'Then they might just as well be living the life of a slave or prisoner.'

'Just so, and many unwittingly do,' continued Yang-Chu. 'The ancients understood that life is only a temporary sojourn in this world, and death is a temporary leave. In our short time here, we should listen to our voices and follow our hearts? Why follow other people's rules and live to please others? Is it not better to be free and live your own life, enjoying whatever comes your way to the full?'

'It is so,' said the Emperor. 'For being imprisoned by name or title allows social conventions to lead one away from the natural order of things.'

'Certainly, and concern over whether one is remembered in generations ahead is a wasteful activity, as our present consciousness will not be there to see it. Rather than spend their life letting other people manipulate them just to get a name and a reputation, a person must let their life be guided by their own heart.'

'So one must live without the burdens of fame and recognition,' said the Emperor.

'One must simply live without the self-importance that requires their necessity. For self-importance devises complexity to sustain itself and this runs against the simple and natural order of things. Thus, the more a person feels they must have, the more they feel they must protect what they have. So, unwittingly, they build a prison maze around themselves, one so complex that keys to get out of it are unnecessary.'

'Then how is it possible for a person to regain their freedom?' asked the Emperor.

'By the only means to see one's bondage for what it really is,' answered Yang-Chu. 'Simply to rise above it.'

❡ Having convinced us that we are much less than we really are, the ego measures our value by what our 'busyness' accomplishes. We have become so tied up with what we do, for example, that we view weekends, or time off, as our periodical escape. Yet the complexity of our lives is such that these escapes only lead to the exercise yard of our self-imposed prison. Could we but rise above all the complications in our lives and see that they have been created to satisfy the demands of ego, we would know the absurdity of what reassuring it continually requires of us.

❡ Do we really need the security blanket of electronic luggage to verify our identity? Do we allow the tools and toys of our particular profession to simplify our lives, as they were intended to? Do we need the complexity of systems to ensure that our businesses run smoothly? Do we need the complexity that we create in our relationships? Must we really have the complexity we have in our lives, in order to live. Or is it *simply* that we have allowed ourselves to be convinced that we do? Think how much more energy we use trying to get around something, rather than just getting on with it. In doing so, we complicate the issue.

🌱 Complexity is born out of a belief that things cannot be simple. Seeking to simplify the complexity of whatever stressful concern you may currently have, will initially cause your ego to ridicule you by saying, 'Ah, but that's easier said than done.' No, it isn't. Try it. Allow yourself to become aware of something being unnecessarily complex. Feel what would be the clearest and simplest solution. Again your ego will say, 'But that's too obvious to work.' Then just do it, and importantly, be aware of how easy it is. If something sounds right to you, because deep down inside it *feels* right to you, then do it. Act on it.

🌱 If something goes against the grain, however, dismiss it. But in doing so be aware of why you are dismissing it. To dismiss something is fine, but to not know why you do so is allowing the ego to say, 'Go on; convince me.' Whatever is true does not need to be defended; it only has to be remembered. Whenever something *feels* right, it is because you already know it to be right. It is just that you have been reminded. Acting in this manner allows you to simplify the complexity in your life. We complicate things more out of fear, than anything else. Fear, the ego's main tool to convince us to meet its demand, leads us to the key to overcoming it.

Fearful Love

✗ Perhaps it is because the world equates business and career success with personal success; and honours the wealthy and accomplished, that the fear of failure is one of the most common and powerful forces in the workplace. When things are going well for us, we do not believe they will last. So rather than simply monitor what we are doing, we begin to complicate things in the belief that, without our increased active interference, our success will not continue. Inevitably, because of our interference, we begin to bring about what we are afraid of.

✗ For example, two people of equal ability embark on separate transactions. Both do all that is necessary for them and to the best of their abilities. One, however, perceives the outcome of their transaction as vital, in terms of income, recognition and self-esteem. The other has no such attachments and, having done all that is possible, begins to think about the next transaction. While the latter monitors progress, the former interferes, tweaking things here and there.

✗ The paradox of success is that the harder you push for something, the further it will move in the other direction. The person who pushes the chain has no control over the links, and they travel in all directions. The person in control is the person who pulls the chain straight. This principle is the same for the leadership of people. Pushing people to do what your ego considers they ought to do is not as effective as them following you, compelled to by your example.

✠ All fears, including the fear of failure and the fear of success, are misguided beliefs that rob us of our peace of mind and upset our lives, spawned by the ego which wants us to forget our own inherent self-worth. We have forgotten that we are divine beings, created to perform the exact opposite of fear and so with the power to miraculously transform all difficult situations we encounter. Creating the exact opposite of fear is aligned to our true-self, and what is the exact opposite of fear? It is certainly not courage, although it takes courage to apply it. It is the compassion one feels for one's fellow beings, the very substance that makes our lives worth living – it is love.

✠ The very word love will always conjure up different meanings for people. When sincerely meant, saying 'I love you' is, for many, one of the hardest things to say. In those few words we open ourselves up to share something with another that leaves us vulnerable. Mentioning such a word in the business arena, apart from in the context of 'I love my work,' is simply not appropriate, considered the worst of all that is associated with that 'touchy-feely stuff.' That is because, in not understanding what love involves, we have allowed our egos to compartmentalise it into something that it is not, something that is just not done in public.

✴ Where fear is about closing ourselves up, love is about opening ourselves up. But in the world of business particularly, we have learned to fear the very opposite of what keeps us in our fearful status quo. Indeed, in all situations we seem to fear love, sticking instead to that which is more familiar to us. Thus, we take more than we give in the belief that giving means to sacrifice and lose something. The world tells us that what we have is diminished if we give, yet to receive more we must give more, and the best thing we can learn to give is love. But the love we must learn to give is not the love that we generally associate with the term, the limited or conditional love we habitually extend to a particular person or thing. It is a divine and unconditional love that reaches beyond what is familiar to us.

✴ Our reason for being is the fulfilling of our potential through the learning and teaching of unconditional love. For it is only through love that we can truly grow. It is what we were created for and is the path essential for fulfilling our potential. But loving our unfamiliar neighbour does not mean that we open ourselves up to abuse from them. It does not mean having to like them, or to put up with inadequate work or disrespectful behaviour from them, as our ego will immediately suggest. It is therefore important to understand what is meant by unconditional love.

✴ Most of us have experienced the meaning of unconditional love, if only for a fleeting moment. At the moment of an offspring's birth, a parent will feel unconditional love. A father holding his son for the first time is filled with an overwhelming sense of joy. Fascinated by his child's vulnerability and dependency he promises to do everything necessary to give him a good life. He will obviously not consider a contract of conditional love, whereby he will look after them *only* on the condition that he receives love, appreciation and gratitude in return.

✻ Yet, a form of conditional love soon begins within the relationship. The father may even make his son feel guilty for the father himself not having fulfilled his own promise to his son. In time the father and son may hardly meet each other lovingly. The son goes to the father when he needs money and the father goes to the son when he wants to give a sermon. The habit of loving conditionally forms as the father becomes increasingly afraid of interaction.

✻ It is because we are only prepared to love according to conditions that we are afraid of falling in love. As frightened people, we seek to make everything secure, according to our ego's conditions, looking for those things which our loved ones wouldn't do if they really loved us. Is it any wonder, therefore, that we consider it almost impossible to love whatever is uncomfortable or beyond what is familiar to us? 'Love your neighbours as your *self*' isn't allowed a moment's thought, let alone 'love your enemies.'

✻ The only way to love your neighbour as your own self is to see your own self in that person. That follows our prime purpose of self-discovery, for it is not possible to see your self in another if you don't know your own self. Since to love is inherent in our creation, the way to self-discovery is to learn and teach unconditional love. In doing so, we begin to remember who we really are. And when we begin to see our selves in others we no longer view them as enemies.

�**ϒ** As the best way to learn something is to teach it, the best way to learn love is to teach love. This validates the truism that the only way to receive love is to give love. Learning to love unconditionally creates miracles, for any miracle is simply an act of unconditional love. All of us are given the opportunity to create miracles in our lives, every hour and every day, simply through treating others as we ourselves would want to be treated. We don't always take the time to, but when we do we are treating others unconditionally. In doing so, we clarify our own thinking because we have dispersed our own fears.

�**ϒ** Choosing to love and forgive another who has offended us, is acknowledging that they are also learning like us. It may be that we have to dismiss another, divorce another, terminate a situation or take legal action against another. But in doing so from love, rather than judgement, we end the personal pain and stress that such action and conflict has previously put us through. It is not possible to predict what miracle will come about from our acting out of love rather than anger towards another.

�**ϒ** The offending person may change or not, but when love has been allowed to enter the situation, things do happen. It may be, for example, that acting through love towards someone we previously resented and judged actually results in our physical removal from them due to a miraculous change in circumstances. They, or we, may be transferred or choose another job. What happens to resolve our difficult situations is later viewed as a wonderful set of beneficial coincidences.

✶ Introducing love into a problematical situation is about reducing the fear within ourselves. It is not learning to love someone we do not even like. Everyone benefits when we release our fears and are able to live more in peace with ourselves. When a person says that they love one person but hate another, they do not know what love is. For love is not limited, it is divine and unlimited. When we respond from love, we respond from our true nature and allow our Divine Will, not our human will, to affect the results. In doing so we harness the most powerful force in the Universe. One that always offers peace, instead of conflict.

✶ There may be someone currently in your life that is causing you a difficulty. It may be someone who always seems to make things difficult for you on purpose, either personally or professionally. Begin to think of them with love, forgiving them for their behaviour and actions towards you. This is admittedly difficult because you have to send loving thoughts, rather than vengeful, aggressive ones. But know that despite the unjustness of the way they are acting towards you, their actions are based on their own insecurities. Accept that they are acting the way they do because they are afraid, frightened, insecure and isolated. They are merely operating from an ego that has convinced them that you are a threat, and must be put in your place under their control.

✯ When you actively do this, you will soon sense strength within you that you did not feel before. You will know that you will overcome whatever difficulty they present without letting it affect you. In this way, you take charge of how things will turn out. In due course, the situation will resolve itself in a way that you had not previously imagined.

✯ This does require courage, but the only way you will resolve your fears is through addressing them with love, unconditionally. Our ego-self acts through fear, our true-self, acts through love. When people bring up your flaws, you resent them for it; but when a good mirror reflects your ugliness, you consider it to be good mirror. Learning to deal with others without involving your ego, will always avoid you being dragged down by them.

Quantum Improvement

✯ Freedom from the ego involves being aware of the continuous attractions it puts in front of us – external desires that serve only to distract us from being our true-self. It means resolving to regain our natural inheritance through acknowledging that there is a source of oneness that we all emanate from. It means reducing the complexity of our life, removing the trivia that we have allowed to insidiously fill our lives, under the misguided belief that it is fulfilling. It means accepting that our primary purpose is to learn, and teach, an unconditional love. It means understanding that no-one is in our life by accident, that they provide opportunities for us to grow into our true-self.

✤ How we express ourselves, through the work which we choose to do, is by far the best arena to develop ourselves, because business brings out the worst expression of the ego. It does so because it involves what we earn, our credibility, our position in society, our social standing, our esteem, and above all, our fears and insecurities. All elements of the workplace offer great opportunity for the ego to fully express itself. The culture of a business, whether a small company or large organisation, is the manifestation of how people think and feel; thoughts and feelings *emanating* from egos.

✤ The greater the level of control for control's sake within the members of a company the smaller their level of self-confidence and self-esteem. When the former goes up the latter goes down, and all other factors, including interpersonal communication, credit seeking and vying for position are influenced accordingly. Fortunes continue to be spent on initiatives in order to improve culture and alter 'the way things are around here'. Most, however, never consider the greatest source from which insecurities, cynicism, scepticism and other impediments, emanate.

✤ Seeking to gain freedom from the ego through recognising its detrimental influence and regaining mastery over it, thus harnessing it as a useful tool, will cause a quantum improvement in how any organisation operates. Addressing the ego will dramatically maximise returns and minimise overheads while at the same time developing rock-solid customer and client relationships. Like any continuous improvement initiative its process is never-ending, but the benefits are priceless to everyone involved, both measurably and immeasurably.

�`⚡` Such a quantum improvement will mark the difference between those individuals who work for the sake of themselves and those who work for the sake of others. The belief that business is different to life in general is a myth. Doing unto others before they do it to you, and treating the person behind the desk differently from the customer in front of the desk, is no longer sustainable. Is it any wonder that the majority of businesses do not see maturity? In the evolving business arena, those leaders who are influenced and driven by the limited and restrictive beliefs of the ego, will not bear fruit as abundantly as those leaders who have mastery over the ego, free from all limited and restrictive thinking.

✝ In the evolving business arena the difference between the two alternatives is becoming increasingly noticeable. Being yourself and gaining whatever you want through building your success on the success of others follows the natural order of things. Getting whatever you want through building your success on the backs of others does not.

✝ The Chinese monkeys, who have philosophically seen no evil, heard no evil and spoken no evil for centuries, are a good example of how to master what is detrimental to us. It is the mischievous and chattering ego within us, however, that we must free ourselves from, in order to embrace the business spirit so essential for success and meaning. When we become aware of perceiving it, of how we listen to it and how we give it voice, it is actually in our interest to shoot, metaphorically speaking, the monkey within us. The leaders, the achievers, the new 'Greats', who do so, will be taking a quantum leap in both their personal and professional lives.

Guiding the Horse

Governing Your Willpower

*T*he horse reared in fright as the shrouded man walked unexpectedly onto the path and startled it.

'Ho there,' cried the carriage driver, struggling to regain control of his animal. 'What devil does such a thing! What do you think you are doing suddenly appearing like that?'

'In peace, I am no devil, moreover, if there were a demon it is within your hand, creating a rein of terror upon unsuspecting travellers,' answered the man.

'You are either a sage or a simpleton, speaking as you do,' said the carriage driver. 'The former, I'll wager, for any fool can see that this powerful horse has been finely trained and is well harnessed.'

'Of what good is the strength of a horse and the control of a harness, if the direction of the will guiding the driver's hand is elsewhere?' said the sage. 'It is clear that you are on this road against your will.'

'What nonsense do you speak of?' retorted the carriage driver, wondering how the sage had hit upon the truth with his last remark. 'Explain yourself, or you'll feel the lash of more than my tongue!'

'The fine carriage in which you sit can be likened to the body; the powerful horse to your feelings and desires; you, as driver, are like the mind; and your will is the master of them all. Will is the development of a wish, the command that turns a wish into action. It is clear that you have no wish to travel wherever you now go, because your will was not ready for the unexpected. The unexpected is the test of true constancy, Man's self-governing key. You did not wish this trip, so, your will lacked the tenacity, steadfastness, stability and fortitude that a road such as this demands. A resolute will has power, control and direction working together. When man lacks this unity, his lack of will is plain for all to see, no matter how he may disguise it.'

'In truth, I have no desire to make this trip,' said the carriage driver. 'But the will of my master is such that I have no choice, though in my heart I know misfortune will come of the business I am ordered to do.'

'It is indeed far easier to train a wild beast than educate one's own will to perform, because of Man's uncertainty as to what he really wants,' replied the sage. 'That is why Man continues to yield the power of his own will to the will of others and calls it destiny.'

⅄ Our will is the greatest power available to us and the very element that determines our success or failure. Will is the basis of our power of constancy, the virtue that encapsulates our tenacity, steadfastness, determination, resolution, perseverance, and fortitude; the basis of our zeal, faithfulness and devotion to that which is important to us. The education and formation of our will plays a much more important role in our success, or failure, than the education and formation of our intellect. Yet, amazingly, the development of our will is left to merciless chance.

✱ The reason that one person succeeds to every ten that fail in business is because the factors that are necessary for the development of an indomitable will are not recognised, understood or applied. Our whole educational system is based on developing the brain in proportion to the amount of intelligent exercise and use to which it is put. But the education that is overlooked is the strength of constancy and will necessary for life's path. The person, who has education, qualifications, rank and position, yet lacks constancy, lacks a great deal in life. The person who lacks money may miss out on certain things in life, but the person who lacks willpower misses everything in life.

✱ There is inevitably more chance of falling than of rising in life. Few devote their attention to the cultivation of will, and since we have not been taught how to use it, most of us do not know how. Consequently, we float along where the current of the will of others takes us, our own submerged, or drowned, from lack of use.

✱ Unwittingly, in our logical thinking, we divide consciousness from will. In the East consciousness means will and the same word is used for will and freedom. By unconsciously giving up our will, we are effectively giving up our freedom. Destiny is always at work with free-will and free-will with destiny. They are one and the same thing; the difference is one of consciousness. The more we become conscious of our will, the more we see that destiny works around it and that destiny works according to it. And the less conscious we are of that will, the more we see ourselves as subject to destiny.

✴ People generally choose to believe in either destiny or free-will. Often it is a question of temperament and the experience they have had in their lives. Some people have worked, had success and recognised it as the outcome of their work. Others, having worked and not succeeded, believe that there is something holding them back which must be destiny. But whether we believe in destiny or not, we are attracted to knowing more about it, because seeing what the future holds for us is the greatest desire of all.

✴ Each of us is born with a plan to be accomplished in life, together with the talents, strengths and instinctive abilities to achieve it. Each of us is attached to a divine plan, yet we all have the free-will to create our individual plan and thus continually change our destiny. There are, therefore, two aspects of will working through all things in life – an unconscious will and a conscious will. When our free-will and the Divine Will work together, things go smoothly; when they are at odds it is like swimming against the tide.

✴ Developing the indomitable-will available to us requires us to tap into the energy that fuels all we are capable of achieving and infinitely more. It is the power that turns wishes into reality. But to do so effectively it must have three attributes working together. It must have strength, be under control and be properly directed. A weak-will won't get you far if it is not properly directed; a strong-will that is not under control is like a horse without a harness, powerful but unfit for pulling. And the strong-will that lacks proper direction is like the carriage horse reined by a half-hearted driver.

⅄ Will is the guide that must master itself, as it is the very power of our self-direction and the strongest expression of the life-force within each of us. The human-will is as much a living force of nature as is gravity, magnetism or electricity. Learning to cultivate and guide such a force changes the individual from mediocre to outstanding. To do so requires both education and application of Determined Willingness, Disciplined Persistence and Decisive Intent. These three keys are the basis of developing the power of constancy and self-government.

Determined Willingness

'What if they say no? If only I didn't have to worry so much about things. Why can't life be more generous?'

'It can, Han Yen,' said Yen Tzu overhearing his nephew talking to himself. 'You simply have to be determined about what you ask for and be willing to sacrifice in order to receive.'

'Sacrifice what?' said Han, 'I don't have anything to sacrifice.'

'Your willpower always finds a way, for it is the very

functionary of your wishes and knows what to sacrifice when necessary,' began Yen Tzu. *'But when you have many desires, which are really only the primitive stage of wishes, your mind is scattered and your willpower deteriorates. Only when your desire becomes a firm and definite wish can you develop with your willpower. But you have to know what you want, or your misguided-will may deliver to you that which you did not expect.*

'There was once a man, for instance, who deep in thought about how he could improve his lot, walked into the jungle. Becoming tired, he found a beautiful tree and sat beneath it. But he couldn't lie down anywhere because the ground was so thorny. "How nice it would be if I had a bed to rest on," thought the man, and no sooner had he done so than he found himself lying down on one. "Yi! This is magnificent. A very comfortable bed to rest on, but I am so hungry I could eat anything. Certainly a banana would be nice." Immediately a bunch of bananas appeared.

"'What's this? I can't believe my eyes. It seems that whatever I want, I get here. Right then, how about some gourmet cooking?" Immediately, plates filled with choice delicacies appeared. Eating sumptuously the man thought, "Ah, how nice it would be for someone to massage my tired feet so that I could fall asleep." Even as he thought of it, there was already a beautiful angel massaging his feet. Now really excited, the man thought, "By the gods this is fantastic! Whatever I'm thinking, I'm getting. Now I have a comfortable bed, a good sumptuous meal and somebody to massage my feet. But what if, while I'm getting the massage, I fall asleep and suddenly a tiger comes

from the jungle. What will happen?" Immediately he heard the roar, and a tiger appeared and devoured him.'

'How crazy to have found such a gift and wasted it so!' said Han Yen.

'Exactly so,' said Yen Tzu, 'but such is the thinking of many. Despite walking into the jungle thinking about what he wanted, his willpower lacked constancy and soon began to desire just basic comforts. If you were to find the fabled boon-giving tree that is ready to give you anything, what would you ask? It won't give it to you until you ask and if you ask for bitter fruit, then that will be your destiny.'

'But I would only ask for that which I knew would be in my best interests,' protested Han Yen.

'Ah nephew,' said Yen Tzu, 'but indeed what are they? For your earlier thoughts, even spoken out loud to strengthen them, were all about worry.

�**✦** Often the meaning of fables is lost. The boon-giving tree, that place to go, think what you want and get it, has been transformed over the centuries into the Christmas Tree, a once-a-year tree with all the gifts underneath. Somehow, our thinking has evolved the view that we should not ask for things, or expect what we want to be given to us. Not choosing to look beyond the meaning of 'ask and you will receive', we hope for the best, while expecting the worst.

✦ Having determination for something is of no use on its own. Neither is perseverance, nor personal drive. These concepts are not the keys to bring what we want into reality. The cries of, 'I really gave it everything I had' or 'Even after persevering for ages, nothing happened' and 'Never mind, you did the best you could have done', may all have the determination, perseverance and personal drive behind them. But there is still something lacking from the state of mind necessary to bring about what is wanted. That key factor is for us to be *willing* to do whatever is necessary.

��� Whenever a person resolutely determines something and is truly willing to do what is necessary, regardless of obstacles, the indomitable-will becomes active. Whatever is asked in such a way is received, for absolutely nothing can resist a willing faith. That willing faith is the boon-giving tree, and each of us holds the roots of it within us. What is required is to feel strongly enough about what we want, in order that willing branches can bear fruit. Being willing is a measure of the rightness of your wish or dream. How much something feels right to you, is in direct proportion to how willing you will feel about working towards it. Whenever you feel unwilling about what you think is right for you, it is a clear indication that it is not.

✣ Being willing to work eight hours a day on achieving something which requires a willingness of eighteen hours a day, for example, is not about doing what it takes. But the amazing thing about willingness is that holding the thought is usually enough. Paradoxically, it does not require greater effort, for the power of will is such that, if one has sufficient willingness, one can find anything one wants to find.

✝ Like the stories of archaeologists, historians, researchers and scientists, for example, all of whom hold an uncompromising willingness. They come across what they are looking for almost as soon as they start looking. In other words, they are guided towards it. It is the same with the poet, the musician, the thinker. When they are deeply interested in what they are doing, then they only have to wish, and by the automatic action of their wish – the will – what they want comes to light.

✝ Similarly, willing business entrepreneurs will streak ahead of other leading organisations in an industry, because their will has made possible that which was considered impossible. When both free-will and Divine Will, usually unstuck by half-heartedness, becomes fused by your willingness, providence literally guides you towards your objective.

✝ Determined willingness is providence itself and is harnessed simply through a certainty that what you want is in harmony with your conviction. Individuals with determined willingness do not acknowledge what others refer to as bad luck. But as ninety-nine out of every hundred people are never clear as to what they really wish, it is not possible for them to develop either determination or willingness. Development of both attributes comes when you are clear about what you desire, so that the powerful-will, the controlled-will and the directional-will work in unison to manifest the object of your desire.

✝ Of the remaining ninety-nine people who are undecided about their desires, some analyse them until they are destroyed; some adopt a passive attitude based on the belief that it is a sin to desire; some hold desires but lack the determination to turn them into a wish, the undeveloped state of will, thus keeping their desires in their primitive stage; and some turn their desires into firm wishes and act on them, but only for the time they perceive it should take, thus being unwilling to do whatever it takes.

✝ The reality of life is that absolutely no-one can exist in the world without wishing for something. Man is great or small, wise or foolish, on the right or wrong road, according to the desire he has. What makes a strong or weak-will is a greater or lesser permanence of desires and wishes. It is fundamentally crucial, therefore, to do whatever it takes to discover what it is we really wish to do with full willingness. If not, knowing that there is more we can do, mediocrity and frustration always follow us. Daily practice of recognising what you are both willing and determined enough to see through is required, and this leads us to the second key.

Disciplined Perseverance

Passing through a forest on his way back from Ch'u, a Patriarch saw a hunchback catching cicadas with a sticky pole.

'What skill you have,' he exclaimed. 'How you seize those elusive flying insects as easily as though grabbing them with your hand! What special way have you learned to do such a thing?'

'I have a way,' replied the hunchback. 'For the first five or

six months I practice balancing two balls on top of each other at the end of the pole and, if they don't fall off, I know I will lose very few cicadas. Then I balance three balls and, if they don't fall off, I know I'll lose only one cicada in ten. Then I balance four balls and, if they don't fall off, I know it will be as easy as grabbing them with my hand. I hold my body like a stiff tree trunk and use my arm like an old dry limb. No matter how huge heaven and earth, or how numerous the ten thousand things, I'm aware of nothing but cicada wings. So, how can I help but succeed?'

The Patriarch turned to his disciples and said, 'See how a Man's spirit concentrated through disciplined perseverance keeps his will undivided. Such power of constancy makes even the impossible look easy!'

𝄐 We are all capable of persisting. Each of us has displayed our natural ability to steadfastly persist when taking our first step. Learning to walk takes courage, determination, self-discipline and perseverance. Yet for too many these natural attributes begin to disappear from lack of use. The 'do I have to' and 'can't someone else do that' syndrome is soon born, strengthened by the appeasement of others.

𝄐 Winners are people who work at doing things that the majority of people are not willing to do. Not being willing to do something, does not mean not being able to do something. Every day there are incredible success stories of individuals who, seemingly unable to be or do, because of disability, adversity, or poverty, overcome all. They win through because their willingness has developed the discipline and persistence to do so.

✱ Without discipline the will still exists. However, in its uncontrolled state it operates as wilfulness, a form of stubbornness exerted when one is not willing to do something that one is capable of doing. Wilfulness is unchannelled will-power, undisciplined-will. When we do not develop the discipline to harness it, then it most assuredly works against us, although we may not be aware of it. Like the stubborn horse that will not be guided away from the path of an oncoming train because it has not finished a tasty morsel growing on the track, our wilfulness too can cause us to be run over.

✱ Often wilfulness is more noticeable in the very young or very old, because the channel to direct it is lacking. A child will insist that a drink stays precariously on the edge of a table; an aged person will insist that certain possessions are zealously kept in place.

✱ But as discipline is a very personal factor, many people lack persistence; they are only willing to do just what is necessary. That is why we marvel at those individuals who do succeed, but rather than acknowledge the years of discipline and persistence it has taken them, our tendency is to give credit elsewhere. Thus, the outstanding athlete is extra talented; the successful person in business had extra support, backing, luck or ruthlessness; the talented musician plays an extra quality instrument; and so on. People will always seek to find another reason for not accepting that they themselves lack discipline and persistence. The fact is, however, that our characters and potential can never reach their best until they are re-channelled with these natural attributes.

✝ Developing discipline means choosing to be firm with yourself until what you are undertaking becomes a habit. Thus, rising an hour earlier to train, study or work at something that you have promised yourself you will do until it is complete, is discipline. If what you are doing requires early rising for years and you stick at it for just weeks or months, then what you are involved with is of only temporary interest to you, a fad. Developing perseverance does not mean sticking to the same thing forever, but it does mean going through the trials and errors of what you want to achieve. It means giving full concentration and effort to the moment. It means doing the hard things first and finishing them before the easy things. It means going that extra mile to achieve what is important to you.

✝ Where discipline maintains the habit to do what you have undertaken, perseverance sustains the strength of the habits. Habitually practising whatever you are willing to be or do, with the enjoined quality of disciplined perseverance, is the vital ingredient that has developed every past, present or future champion.

✝ The evolving business world increasingly demands that individuals embark on what they do with discipline, accepting such a way as a personal responsibility. This is, of course, how things should be, but is not so in reality. Most discipline is used to control one person by another for obedience purposes, rather than for developing constancy within the individual. With constancy, external obedience is not necessary, as people recognise the importance and observe the power of how individual wills can work together for common purpose.

✙ To develop such discipline first requires matching the right talents and strengths with the appropriate responsibilities. Making others do something that they are clearly unwilling to do is setting discipline against stubbornness, which is not in the interest of our family, group, team or company. Obviously, you have to be sure that the stubbornness is not in fact laziness, but strengthening round wheels with square pegs is a measure that will ultimately distort the wheel and make the ride rough for everyone. As our natural tendency is to do whatever is easiest first, and then procrastinate over what is clearly the hardest task, it is obviously best to focus high priority work on the most productive areas which will further develop disciplined perseverance.

✙ When we are choosing of our own volition to persist in doing more than we are asked and contribute more than is required, we become able to expect the unexpected. When we come to expect the unexpected we are ready for anything. Confident in the strength of our discipline we remain unconcerned, irrespective of what we may have to suddenly deal with.

✝ With our persistence being the measure of our belief in ourselves, we readily engage and successfully overcome whatever obstacles may appear before us. Becoming a disciple of persistently practising discipline leads us to achieve what we formerly believed impossible. When we achieve to this extent, a state of calm certainty is experienced which opens up our skills to using the final key.

Decisive Intent

'What is meant by the saying "The one who turns his back on the world hears the whole world run after him"?' asked Second Merchant Lee Mok.

'This can be understood from our perspective,' answered First Merchant Fu Jung, 'by watching two people bargaining. A peddler, at Yellow Court market, for instance, comes up to you with an object, and you say how beautiful and intricate it is, that you like it and how much will he take for it. As soon as you have said this, the peddler wants you to give as high a price as he is intent on getting from you.

'Yet, when you turn your back saying that you do not care for it, he comes after you asking if you will take it for half. If you continue turning your back, he will offer it to you for a quarter, or even less. Such is the greedy nature of this world. You follow it, it runs from you; you turn your back on it, it comes after you. Both require intent but, only with decisiveness, will you master the latter.'

'So one must have a decisive intent,' said Lee Mok, 'but how can one attain such a quality in a world of constant persuasions?'

'By developing calm steadfastness and certainty of purpose,'
replied First Merchant Fu Jung. For in truth, having the
inability to decide will put you at the mercy of the many people
who will smell your indecision coming towards them. Even as
though you had slipped in the dung-heap of destiny.'

❡ Life is a series of choices. The quality of both our personal
and working life is a result of our previous decisions. For it is
our decisions, and not our conditions, circumstances,
education, or background that determine our future. As a
species we are unique in our ability to choose to live by the
consequence of either our own decisions, or those of others.
Most of us, however, forfeit the majority of our lives by
choosing the latter, allowing others to decide for us. Many
consistently argue that often there is no choice, but as the
world will accept no neutral, even not choosing is making a
decision. It is choosing to be indecisive.

❡ Being decisive is a fundamental skill that is both learned
and improved through practice. But instead of developing the
skill, many of us unwittingly decide to spend our time
improving our complaining skills over those decisions taken
by others that affect us. Infinitely more time and energy will
be expended by a group discussing someone else's decisions,
than by making them personally. Indeed, the person who is
prone to complain is almost always indecisive.

❡ Without doubt, as a race we can be divided into those
who are decisive, and those who are indecisive. Being in

command and feeling secure in ourselves is part and parcel of being decisive and having a firm intent. People recognise when you have these qualities and chase after you. But they also clearly recognise when you do not, and are able to keep you where they want, or get from you what they want. The degree that we are indecisive is in direct proportion to how insecure we feel, whether consciously aware of it or not.

✶ Being unable to decide means having uncertainty in ourselves, indeed being unable to trust in ourselves. Too many of us, though competent to do anything, end up doing nothing because of our inability to decide. Like Dante's starving man, perplexed at which meal to eat first, our own 'Divine Comedy' is alarming, for the majority of people are unable to decide what life they want to lead, even with all the options laid before them. It is little wonder, therefore, that decisive intent is rare. Yet it is by far the most sought-after quality in leadership and the very ignition that sparks will and sustains constancy. Decisiveness is personal surety.

✶ Developing decisiveness is an essential part of developing will. It is possible to divide the will into three parts: Volitional-Will, Static-Will, and Dynamic-Will. Volitional-Will is that part of the will which moves us to action. Without it there can be no act of will. Deciding to return and finish something you have started, or simply returning to work after lunch, are examples of this element.

✶ To measure the strength of our volitional-will is to observe whether our bodies respond immediately and positively when we decide to do something, rather than ignoring or contradicting our mind's decision. Very simply it is the will that causes you to get out of bed in the morning, when you'd rather not. To want something is not the same as to will it, you may want to speak a language, for example, but if there is no volition to learn it, then you won't.

❧ No volition can be put forth without an expenditure of energy and this is where static-will comes in. This is the part of will that contains the energy for action. It is here that energy is accumulated and stored. The static-will cannot be engaged without volition, and neither can a volitional-will be enacted without drawing its energy from the static-will. To measure our static-will's strength we should observe the level of mental listlessness, or resistance, when involved in something which does actually interest us.

❧ When volitional-will and static-will have joined together to set a course of action into motion, dynamic-will ensures its completion. It is that part of the will that does not give up. Its strength can be measured by observing how consistent our efforts are in following our decisions through. All three parts of will form an energy cycle that keeps us moving forward. Static-will accumulates energy, providing it to the dynamic-will, which expends it in a series of co-ordinated and concerted individual volitions.

❧ The real test of intent always comes down to the strength of the volitional-will, which means the ability to make choices, preferences, discernments and decisions. The degree to which you allow yourself to remain indecisive is in direct proportion to the low reserves of energy in the static-will, and infrequent spurts from the dynamic-will.

✦ Thus, the less we make decisions, the less we are inclined, and the less energy we have. Even when we make decisions, we will lack the energy to see them through. Subsequently, we lack steadfastness and calmness of purpose, tending to wait for something to happen rather than make it happen. Without decisiveness, the remaining energy of our will is channelled into procrastination, complacency and apathy, causing us to complain and worry.

✦ There are two simple keys to becoming decisive. One is continual practice and the other is to take absolute responsibility for the outcome of your decisions, irrespective of the consequences. Developing decisive-intent goes further. It means taking ownership of your intent being fully accountable for all outcomes, even if what you decide is delegated to another to perform. It does not mean looking for the out before you start, like a prenuptial contract. It means accepting that, even if everything is on the line, you still win because your decision is in harmony with your values, conviction and fundamental beliefs.

Duty to Resolve, Will and Decide

✦ Both will-power and decisiveness are as vital to each other as yin and yang. They are complementary parts essential to their greater whole. *Resolving to will to decide* something, therefore, is the simple key to overcoming indecision and developing an iron-clad will. An indomitable-will is that *useful* part of the ego discussed in Lesson four. The education and development of the will is one of the objects of our existence, for everything becomes possible when a person says I *will*, with all the force, energy and determination of his or her character.

✠ In turn there can be no finer way to build our character, as gaining mastery over each attribute of will develops strength in the others. Thus, willingness builds discipline; discipline builds perseverance; perseverance builds decisiveness; and decisiveness strengthens willingness. Similarly, volitional-will builds static-will, which in turn drives dynamic-will and strengthens even the silent-will, that unseen force of intent, truth and goodness, that nothing can resist.

✠ It is our willpower which ignores all the odds, regardless of the fact that they seem stacked against you. Our strength of will distinguishes an individual as surely as muscle power distinguishes the strongest stallion. And our power of constancy, the key to self-governing success, encapsulates all the elements of will, discipline and decisiveness. Ensuring that we develop such power and energy to the full is more than our personal responsibility, it is our very duty that we each owe to ourselves as human beings.

The human will, that force unseen,
The offspring of a deathless soul,
Can hew a way to any goal,
Though walls of granite intervene.
You will be what you will to be,
Let failure find its false content,
In that poor word, environment,
But spirit scorns it and is free.

It masters time, it conquers space,
It cows that boastful trickster, chance,
And bids the tyrant circumstance
Uncrown and fill a servant's place.
There is no chance, no destiny, no fate,
Can circumvent, hinder, or control,
The firm resolve of a determined soul.
Gifts count for nothing, will alone is great,
All things give way before it, soon or late.

What obstacle can stay the mighty force
Of the sea-seeking river in its course,
Or cause the ascending orb of day to wait?
Each wellborn soul must win what it deserves,
Let the fools prate of luck. The fortunate
Is one, whose earnest purpose never swerves,
Whose slightest action, or inaction serves
That one great aim. Why, even Death itself
Stands still and waits an hour sometimes
For such a will. Anon

Riding the Tiger

Channelling Your Energy

'*T*oday my elder son, Ni, joins us,' said Merchant Hui Neng proudly, to all the agents and workers gathered together. 'Ni has studied under many teachers who assure me that he will prove to be our most valuable asset.'

Having built up his business from nothing, Hui Neng had been determined that his eldest son would not be deprived of a good all-round education. For Ni's part there had been many lessons. He had excelled at rhetoric and debate, which he'd really enjoyed, and was able to express himself eloquently. But he had done so badly at his figure work that his tutors had decided to replace debating studies with twice the amount of figure work.

'You will not be able to join your father in business without figure work,' advised his tutors. 'Just because you dislike it is no excuse to shirk.'

'But why must I study what is of no interest to me at the expense of what does interest me?' argued Ni.

'Because that is the way you will become stronger,' they had answered stubbornly. 'Redoubling your efforts on your lesser skills is the only way to remove your weaknesses.'

So, over the next few years, Ni was forced to redouble his efforts, yet, despite working twice as hard, he still received mediocre results. His tutors, however, were pleased to see that he questioned their authority less and less, and that he became more of a critic in the few debates they did allow him to participate in. They were content when they announced to his father that, in their opinion, Ni was ready to enter business, for they had succeeded in teaching Ni the importance of eliminating weakness.

'He will be one of your greatest assets', they told him. 'Your business will continue to grow in strength under your son's careful eye.'

Ni immediately began to replicate the methods he had learned, and for the first time in twenty years his father's business began to lose money.

⅄ All of us are mediocre at many things, are good at some, excel at fewer and have the ability to become world-class at something. This is because for every natural strength we are born with, we have countless weaknesses. Having a strength is not the opposite of having a weakness, however. Like success and failure, or health and illness, each follows a particular pattern.

⅄ Where experiencing failure may be the stumbling block on the natural path to success, seeking improved strength through fixing weakness is very much the wrong path. Fixing weaknesses to improve an individual or business is a fallacy. None the less, it is a practice that is consistently applied throughout schools and all forms of business - to find out what is weak and to ensure its removal through concentrated effort – a practice based on the *misguided* belief that existing strengths will continue to develop on their own; and to become the most effective you can be, spend more time on those areas holding you back.

✿ Everyday the majority of business managers spend time reviewing or appraising others within their control. This is in accordance with the established frame of reference which dominates business thinking – management controls people and things. To control people you monitor their efficiency and effectiveness. The measurement for these elements is the appraisal or review, both good mechanisms, but as the thinking behind them is wrong they are inefficient and ineffective. This is a sweeping yet true statement, as the way they are carried out wastes the time and skill of both appraiser and the appraised.

✿ When a company starts out it is able to concentrate on its strengths; once it is established its focus of attention is on correcting its weaknesses. When a child is very young parents are delighted about what their offspring can do; as the child gets older the parents are concerned at what he or she cannot do. Starting school, both parents and teachers focus on discussing what a child is good at. Later, both focus on the lowest marks in a report. The established thinking is firmly set in a frame of reference that is programmed to root out weaknesses in ourselves and others. In considering your own habits for example, you will recall your bad ones more quickly than your good ones. Consider your strengths and weaknesses. Which come to mind first?

✔ With our thinking rooted in improving what's wrong, the majority of our energy is spent in that area. Every day we have a certain amount of energy: physical, emotional, mental and psychic, in ascending order of importance, our psychic energy being the most valuable. When attention is directed to what we can't do, rather than to what we can do, we unwittingly drain ourselves of our psychic energy. Chastising ourselves mentally for being bad at something, for example, will cause us to feel mentally perplexed, emotionally frustrated and physically tired.

✔ Conversely, praising ourselves for excelling at something will cause us to be mentally stimulated, emotionally euphoric and physically energetic. This situation is rare, however, because our belief is that if you point out weaknesses and fix them, then everything will be all right. Nothing could be further from the truth, even though your rationale will be shouting at you, saying: 'But you have to know what is wrong, how else can you learn to excel?' The truth is that trying to succeed in an area where you are weak will cause you to develop low self-esteem, a poor self-image and a limited self-ideal. These are the elements that make up your self-concept, the most important command centre you have in your life. Is it any wonder that self-acceptance is lost, when we have been trained to focus our attention on what we must do to correct ourselves, rather than what we can do to excel?

✝ Learning to recognise our strengths and developing the courage to channel our energy into developing them, will transform us into the excellent human beings we were born to be. Those who learn how to successfully channel their energy will be the leaders and achievers in their specific fields. Those who don't will continue to feel the inner frustration associated with being unfulfilled.

✝ Entrenched thinking cannot simply be eliminated, as nature abhors a vacuum. It must be replaced with different thinking, frames of reference that work for you, not against you. Practising the following keys will strengthen, rather than develop, these frames of reference, because their very application will serve to remind you of their soundness.

SOM Up vs SWOT Down

'You said that these measures would generate growth, yet all they have done is slow up the growth we previously enjoyed,' said a perplexed Hui Neng to his son. 'This past year we have diverted all of our resources into shoring up our weaknesses, as you said it would make us more efficient and our people more effective, yet now even Agent Jong has stopped producing.'

'It is simply part of the process,' replied Ni. 'The numerous weaknesses that we have addressed will inevitably make us stronger, but it takes time. As for Agent Jong, I have worked long and hard on improving his figure work, to the point at which his orders can quickly be referenced and measured. They may be less than before, but this is normal. As soon as

his productivity in the field increases again, after his training, he will be a good example to others on how to maintain his figures.'

'But Jong was my first agent,' said Hui Neng, 'I have known and accepted his methods for years and everyone loves him. Indeed many of our customers are so, only because of Jong. It seems to me that your teaching has impeded him from building his relationships.' Hui Neng paused and looked at his son. He remembered how the young Ni used to love going around with Jong. The agent would say how his son used to talk and laugh with the customers. Something had changed. 'I have a simple philosophy which has always worked,' he continued. 'Work hard, but only at what you love. If struggle is needed, do not do it, for it is not for you. It does not seem right to me for us to spend so much time evaluating our weaknesses and threats.'

'We don't,' argued his son. 'Using the method of analysis that I learned, we look at Strengths, Weaknesses, Opportunities and Threats.'

'That may be the theory, Ni, but the reality is that your whole focus is on our weaknesses and threats. Little time is spent considering what we are good at.'

'That's because we have so many weaknesses and threats!' replied Ni. 'Father, we must correct what we are not good at and concern ourselves with our competitors, or, we will be lost.'

✝ Imagine a plain wall as a metaphor for a well run, successful business. Now imagine that there is a tiny mark somewhere on it. Where do you focus your attention? It travels to the mark. The established thinking of 'let's fix what's wrong' has become so obsessive that we can spot a flaw in seconds, simply because that is what we are looking out for. Whenever someone makes a presentation, we are more attuned to its weaknesses than its strengths. Whenever we meet someone, we are more attuned to evaluating what we dislike about them, rather than what we may like. How many times are we missing the good by habitually searching for the bad?

Take the SWOT analysis, which is applied regularly in business. Strengths, Weaknesses, Opportunities and Threats are reviewed and considered, yet, without exception, the categories of weakness will take precedence over what is considered strong. Every report will highlight more of the former than the latter in the sincere, albeit misguided belief that what is wrong must be brought to attention. But it is possible to be sincerely wrong.

For example in researching what keeps families together in the UK, emphasis is placed on resolving the weaknesses that cause break-up, rather than on developing the strengths that bind them. Amazingly, all institutional psychology is based on what makes people depressed, rather than on what makes them happy. Opportunities and strengths are given lip service but are not considered worthy of the same discussion time allotted to weaknesses and threats. In the same way that bad habits come to mind before good habits, it is mistakenly considered prudent to address weaknesses before strengths.

¥ The trouble is that there is never any time to develop the strengths further. This, however, is considered of no great concern, because the erroneous belief is that strengths, left alone, will continue to develop on their own. Far from it. Nature will remove from you whatever you do not use, regardless of the strength of the original gift. No quality can exist without being maintained by what it attracts every moment of the day. Many are born with genius, many with a tendency to write poetry, an inclination to sing, or some other ability. Their gifts vanish, however, if they are starved of use, as do the qualities associated with that gift.

¥ The SWOT analysis can more accurately be termed the 'Seek Weaknesses Only Test'. The manager will spend more time with the salesman over the sales he didn't close, than those he did. He will spend more time with the clerk over the errors he has made rather than discussing the ideas he may have. He will spend more time with the receptionist over procedures of recording than on developing interaction with visitors. Tests are designed to find out what people are not good at, rather than to discover what they are good at. The brilliant practical student is forced to improve his theoretical work, while the brilliant theorist is forced to test his ideas in practical ways which may be out of date. Focusing purely on the strengths of each makes them stronger; focusing on weaknesses makes them weaker. The catalyst may not be a strategist and the strategist is rarely a catalyst, yet together they are considerably stronger than the one who is forced to be both.

✗ The only way to develop strengths and opportunities is to ignore anything else. Applying the Strengths, Opportunities and Merits analysis, SOM, will focus the attention on what is, in the end, the only element of any importance. When you identify your strengths and focus solely on them, your weaknesses do not count. In excelling in what you are brilliant at, your weaknesses become unimportant. Athletes ensure that they only train at what they are good at. In doing so they are remembered for what they can do, rather than what they can't do.

✗ This is not the case in the business arena. Strong cash flow is considered to be the life-blood of business, yet it is merely a by-product of the real life-blood. The real life-blood is strong movement of products or services through strong relationships. Relationships are sustained by people who are good at building them because they like what they do. As the need for these people to become experts in compiling and recording data insidiously occupies a growing business, there is less time to move products and build relationships. The regularity of the use of the refrain: 'you can't do that' or 'we need a meeting to discuss it first' is indicative of whether a company is focusing on its weaknesses.

Ni was pleased with himself and he knew that his former tutors would also have been pleased. Having invested a great deal of time with Jong and the other agents, he had finally taught them to correctly fill in their expense sheets, their A reports, their B reports and their C reports. *And they were doing it on time, or almost.* Jong had complained that he'd spent more time on paperwork than on anything else, but Ni had assured him that he would get better at it. Admittedly, income had gone down at first, but that was the marketplace they were in. He had already warned his father that they must diversify rather than specialise, but he would attend to that later. Now, though, income was increasing once more.

'How-so Jong,' hailed Hui Neng, seeing his old friend and agent. 'I see that you are once more winning against the fray. But, hold, why do you look so pleased yet guilty?'

'I am guilty, my lord, because I hold a secret I would prefer to share with you, yet am loath to do so. I am pleased because the purpose behind the secret is worthy.'

'Then my worthy Jong, share the secret with your friend and the guilt will go.'

So Jong explained how for many months now he had struggled with the elements that Ni had introduced. 'Not just I,' he said, 'but all the others, except for Zhang'.

'Zhang?' commented Hui. 'But he has been the laziest of all my agents.'

'Exactly so,' continued Jong, 'but in the matters of form-filling, the duck has taken to the water. So we all devised a plan. Zhang will do everyone's paperwork and we have taken over Zhang's area. He receives his full quota, which was more than he received before, and we are free to do what we love and receive our just reward.'

'And I take it that Ni does not know this?' asked Hui. 'No doubt you are concerned that he will insist that you must all do your own.'

'Exactly so, master, this is why I feel guilty. I have known Ni for all his years, but he has not the light-heartedness that he carried as a child. It is as though he is obsessed with what makes us weak. Yet our plan, you may recognise, is nothing less than how we began. We work on what we are good at...'

'...because we found that anything we were not good at took twice as long for half the reward!' finished Merchant Hui. 'I suppose in the beginning our only assets were our strengths, and we sought to embrace every worthwhile opportunity that our strengths opened up. Today our concern has been more on what others do, rather than what we do. What we do to simplify life actually makes it more complex.'

⅄ No-one likes having fault found with what they do, yet everyone has the inclination to do just that with others. The inclination exists because of the belief that, in finding fault, we are being supportive. Although there is nothing fundamentally wrong in a SWOT analysis, it is the application of it that is self-defeating. Applying the SOM analysis strengthens your thinking. Over the next seven days, apply it to whatever you are involved with, as well as yourself. Only consider strengths and opportunities. Do not even entertain or consider ideas relating to weaknesses or threats of any nature. When appraising another, be they a child, spouse, friend or colleague, ap*praise* their merits, not their faults.

⅄ The main point of this exercise is to place the emphasis of your appraisal on improving what you can do, rather than improving what you can't do. Rather than seek to discover why one team does not communicate or perform, seek to discover why another team does, and plan to do more of it. Rather than seek to learn why people complain, seek to discover why others do not, and follow their example.

✿ When you are conscious of where the emphasis of your thinking is applied, you can then consider weaknesses and threats, as you will place them in their proper perspective - be aware of them so that they do not get in your way. SOMing up rather than SWOTing down allows you to find out what you are good at and do more of it, and to find out what you are not good at so that you can stop doing it. This opens the way to developing the next key. But remember, it is when you juxtapose these simple truths that you complicate your life.

Becoming a Specialist

It is said that the great Sun Tzu was always searching for the world's greatest strategist, right up until he was called to enter the Garden of the Jade Emperor. Indeed, at the very gates the Immortal Guardian, Dragon King Ao-Kuang, welcomed him, exclaiming: 'Ah Sun Tzu, we have been expecting you. The very person for whom you have searched so long and hard has also recently arrived.'

'Do you actually mean the world's greatest strategist? Who? Where?' asked Sun Tzu immediately.

'Look yonder, the person you seek is just over there,' replied the Immortal Ao-Kuang.

Filled with anticipation and excitement, Sun Tzu turned but what he saw dismayed him. 'But what joke is this? Is this hell's gate I have come to? This man cannot be the person I sought so long and so hard for! He is no warrior or leader of men. He was the general boatman on the River Huai in my home state of Wu, and, so they say, a handyman before that.'

'Because he was good at many things,' said the Immortal Guardian, 'he was often called upon by others, and never got down to doing what he would have excelled at. Had he specialised with the talents he had been given by the Jade Emperor, he would have been the greatest warrior strategist who had ever lived. Artfully manoeuvring the dangerous current and courageously saving the lives of many on the River Huai came easily to him because of his gifts.'

Ni's great uncle, Yen Tzu, paused after telling the story, before adding, 'You see, Ni, had the boatman known about his true strengths, or had they been recognised by another, he would have been able to harness them. Had he been aware of them he would not have spent his life diversifying, he would have focused his energy on becoming the specialist that would have fulfilled his capabilities.'

'You have always spoken wise words, Uncle, but surely what you are saying requires you to put all your eggs in one basket? My scholars were adamant about diversifying, as it helped to spread any risk.'

'Ah,' answered Yen Tzu, 'but how many scholars have ever operated a business, let alone successfully? Experiencing the dark night of the soul is not a theory which can have a model built and applied. Business to many of them is something they test their theories on, making it appear more complex than it actually is. Parents with one child will watch their child more carefully than parents with five children. Each child should be watched the same, but there is not the time unless the family works as a team.

'If you only have one basket of eggs you are more careful with that basket. When you have eggs in lots of different baskets you are not so concerned if one basket is lost. When you diversify, where do you spend the fixed amount of energy that one day provides? A bit here and a bit there. When you specialise, you apply all your energy. Always put your eggs in one basket, Ni, and guard that basket well, with all of your energy. In that way your eggs will hatch, grow and multiply.'

'But although what you say appears to be sound,' pressed Ni, 'why is it that so many businesses fail? If they had something else to fall back on, they could see their way through hard times.'

'More businesses fail that have diversified than specialised,' answered his great uncle. 'But there are many reasons that businesses fail, the top of which is that people demand more out of something than they are prepared to put in. Many are impatient, and after trying one thing for a short time become bored and apply their energy in another direction. You talk of the need of your father's business to diversify, when its strength is in the speciality it provides. There is of course nothing wrong with diversifying within the specialisation itself, so long as the core skill remains and does not become incidental to the business. You will find, Nephew, that the strength of a core skill will diminish in proportion to the increase in diversification. A business needs to be nurtured like a child. And *the best way to rear a child is to recognise that it is not an extension of yourself, it is an expression of everything that is good about you.'*

✗ When you truly express yourself, the world embraces the enthusiasm and commitment you display. It applauds your individuality. When you extend yourself the outcome is not always as you would have hoped for. The key to fully expressing yourself is to find out what you love and to specialise in it to the full. Those who do seek to specialise inevitably discover that the rewards are disproportionate between the best and the rest. Similar to the winning horse whose owner receives ten times more than the owner of the horse that came second, the specialist will reap increasing returns for being the best.

✗ Specialisation is perhaps the single most important factor in evolution itself. Every species has a tendency to seek out its ecological calling and develops its strengths accordingly in order to fulfil itself. Man, however, has a tendency to be influenced by artificial circumstances rather than natural conditions. Thus he seeks to adapt and improvise rather than create and develop.

✗ For example, a person may create a speciality that meets a demand and develop a niche market that brings rewards. Later, the very dynamics responsible for the speciality and niche are allowed to be influenced by external factors. The somewhat larger organisation that has evolved because of the original speciality and niche becomes concerned about changing markets, competition or recession cycles. Believing that future survival depends on adapting to changing circumstances it decides to diversify. Unwittingly, however, it begins to weaken itself. Instead of reviewing core skills and expressing them in such a way as to meet the changing demands of the marketplace, it involves itself in the areas in which it lacks strength. Where it was once in command, it is now at the mercy of fluctuations in share and interest rates which lie beyond its control. As it extends its energy in concern about elements beyond its control, it becomes increasingly vulnerable.

✤ To specialise, however, does not mean to restrict the possible range of services or products, as long as they are complementary. A bookshop holding a wide range of books is preferable to a bookshop carrying a restricted selection. Where a firm of lawyers may choose to cater for every eventuality that requires law, an individual lawyer who chooses to do so will inevitably be mediocre. Where a mediocre lawyer mistakes being busy for being successful, a specialist lawyer is in demand regardless of his or her fee. Indeed, regardless of the business, when you are competing with a specialist, your profitability will be determined by the service they offer against yours.

✤ Knowledge, more now than ever before, is the critical ingredient for attaining leadership irrespective of the marketplace. Knowledge provides the edge in specialisation to the extent that if you are not continually learning in your specific subject, then whenever you meet another person who is, they will win, and you won't.

✗ The only place to diversify is within the specific specialisation itself, and, even more effective, only diversify through strategic alliances. There can be no finer way to share risk and increase standards through complementary resources than by forging strategic alliances. This involves the building of relationships which has been discussed in lesson two. The key now, to becoming a world-class specialist, is in channelling your daily energy correctly.

Same Time, Different Choice

✗ The one thing that every person has in common is the amount of time they have in an hour – sixty minutes. Depending on individual priorities, the manner in which these same periods are spent is infinite in choice. Amazingly though, and despite efficient management of time, the majority of our achievement and happiness takes place in a minority of time. Using the unit of one hour as a reference point, ten minutes is utilised in channelling our energy proactively, while fifty minutes is wasted in using our energy reactively. With the majority of our energy absorbed through involvement with such draining elements, it is no surprise that there is so much fatigue and depression.

✗ Every waking hour takes you either towards fulfilling your particular speciality, or away from it. There is no neutral, only forwards or backwards. Channelling your energy has nothing to do with keeping in balance, which is more to do with restoring energy that has been drained. When you channel your energy correctly you actually generate energy; when you do not, you divert energy into frustration, procrastination, exasperation and many other *'ations*. Being in balance means having command over the use of your own energy. This requires spending your time only on those activities that you have previously decided are of high value to you. The fact is, however, that we allow what is actually significant to us to be submerged by whatever is insignificant to us.

✗ Deciding what is important in our lives is very much an individual consideration. But as most people do not know what is important in their lives, prioritising can be impossible. The result is the tendency to live vicariously through others; we become more interested in what others are doing, than in what we ourselves should be doing. A glance at what dominates daily news reports provides ample testament to this tendency.

✗ In applying the rule of *'it is not the hours you put in, it is what you put in the hours'*, consider the following: Do your waking hours involve:

- thinking about what you should have done;
- worrying about what you should be doing;
- doing things other people have asked you do and which you couldn't say no to;
- doing things you don't enjoy;

- doing things that are interrupted;
- doing things you are not very good at;
- doing things that are part of a ritual;
- doing things that are predictable;
- doing things in order to put off what you have planned to do;
- daydreaming about what you would like to be doing.

But that's just the way life is, you may be thinking to yourself. To spend time the way you want, or for that matter ought, is just not feasible. Your work does not allow you the freedom to do otherwise, or you would have to be single to live the way you want. In any case, you think, one must not be selfish. Wrong.

✶ However you rationalise it you will not detract from the reality of the way you currently employ your energy. Becoming a specialist requires more than mere discernment. It demands a firm ruthlessness in saying no to anything that you intuitively feel is draining your energy. This requires real honesty with yourself as to what is important in your life, for it is only with such honesty that you can be honest with others.

✶ In turn this involves establishing ground rules with those you share your life with. Treating others as you yourself would want to be treated, by definition involves thinking of what is right for you first, for when you are on course the ripple effect that exudes from you is beneficial to others. Applying this Golden Rule does not mean you should compromise what is important to you, however, for seeking to please others just so that they will not think ill of you can build resentment and guilt.

✤ It is, of course, difficult to cut out activities that take you away from what you want, when you are uncertain as to what it is you do actually want. But knowing what you want, and doing what you enjoy, are the very pillars of specialisation success. This leads us to the next vitally important key.

Following a Calling

'Running a business is like riding a tiger,' said Merchant Hui Neng to his son. 'There is immense strength and power within your hands and, as you pound through the jungle, your blood races with adrenaline. If you drive the tiger too hard, you run the risk of riding it into the ground, burning out all of its energy. If you ride it too softly, your attention weakens and the tiger, as if sensing your lack of direction, may unexpectedly spring in a different direction, where the jungle is even denser. If you stop, though, the tiger may turn and maul you, leaving you in pieces.'

'I have learned, Father,' said Ni, 'about the importance of developing strengths and of specialising, but how can one ride a tiger without rest, as you say, and still maintain balance?'

'By having a calling, developing a passion and learning to communicate it to others in such a way that they want to support you,' the merchant answered. 'When you are able to align what you do with what you are, you build for yourself unyielding support.'

'But surely only idealists have callings,' said Ni, 'and they are usually empty.'

'That may appear to be so because having a personal mission is so rare,' replied Hui. 'It is rare because society does not

promote it, and it does not do so because it does not understand its importance. Goals to further develop our careers are promoted, but rarely are they encapsulated within the framework of a personal calling. Yet each person's calling, my son, will be the very essence of why they do what they do. The idealist is the sincere individual who follows his ideal, regardless of how others perceive it. A calling is what throws light on the path of life and what gives interest to life. Tell me: If a man does not live for an ideal, what does he live for?'

'For himself, I suppose,' Ni answered.

'Exactly so, and when he lives for himself, he lives for nothing. Whosoever lives and knows not an ideal, is without power and without light. A sincere ideal, no matter how small, is an ideal. The greater the ideal, the greater the person; the deeper the ideal, the deeper the person; and the higher the ideal, the higher the person. Without ideal, calling or mission, whatever the person is in life, their life is causeless.

'Always remember Ni to follow your heart by encapsulating everything that you stand for, everything that is important to you, and everything that is worthwhile to you, into your own personal calling. And, if you do not yet know what that calling is, then make it your first cause to discover it. Hunt your own tiger, mount it and then ride for all you are worth.'

✳ There is nothing more personally motivating, more energy building, more fulfilling and more worthwhile, than knowing that what you do is what is important to you, is what holds meaning for you, is what you want to do, and, above all, is what you are inclined to do.

✹ The best way to channel your energy is to develop your strengths; the best way to develop strengths is to build them within the framework of your own personal mission. Having a calling and following it gives purpose to life and meaning to what you do. Without a personal calling your energy will flow into the countless tributaries of materialistic goals, all of which will sap your strength in due course.

✹ To live and breathe is to be created for a purpose, and to discover and fulfil that purpose is to realise our potential. Moreover, each of us has a responsibility and duty to be extravagant with our potential, for why else would it be given to us? Absorbing ourselves in something bigger and grander than ourselves provides the opportunity to fully develop and share our strengths.

✹ Having a clear purpose allows us to believe in ourselves and know what we stand for; it's about deciding what business you are in as a person. In the same way that you would not have confidence in a business that didn't know what it stood for, why should a company have confidence in an individual who doesn't know what he or she stands for? If you don't know what you stand for, you are continually pulled betwixt and between anything else that comes along.

✹ Discovering your calling and developing it with accompanying values means sticking to a process. This in itself is difficult, as it is both emotionally and spiritually searching. Anything worthwhile does require effort, of course, but it removes the feeling of continual yet futile struggle, as it turns a sense of longing into a sense of belonging. The process requires deep and reflective time alone as only your own intuitive self can provide the answers. By all means crystallise your thinking in discussions with others, so long as you remember that family, friends and colleagues are agencies, not sources.

✦ For a mission to be personal it has to encapsulate the passion of your own vision, not someone else's. Be aware of aligning yourself to something to please or impress others. Too many people live by scripts which have been handed to them by others, with no contribution by themselves.

✦ In asking and answering questions to discover your calling it is important to be aware of being yourself. This means being honest and true to yourself without allowing any rationalisation to cloud your thinking. To the degree that you are yourself, you become receptive to understanding what you are to do. To the degree that you are not true to yourself, you are closed to what you are to do. In answering questions such as 'what difference is my life going to have made?' and 'what would I want others to say of me when I'm gone?', you must be your honest self.

✦ However long it takes, aim to develop a meaningful statement that will galvanise your strengths and talents. Clarify what values are central to your life and work, and ensure that they are reflected in your personal goals, relationships with others, the commitments and promises you make, and the kind of preferences you hold. Established values take the tension out of those decisions which cause the 'will I, won't I' dilemmas.

✝ The process of crystallising your calling in a meaningful statement may take hours, weeks or months. You will also need to regularly review it, but do persevere as the quest for meaning and purpose in your life is far too important to be just fitted in, or to be treated as a task on a 'to do' list. Remember that your calling is something that every fibre of your being yearns for, that excites you emotionally, motivates you mentally and fulfils you spiritually. As such it is of paramount importance.

✝ Having a statement of what is important to you allows you to align what you do with what you are. It qualifies you to assist in developing or reviewing a mission for your company, or the organisation in which you work, with new understanding and appreciation. It is nothing less than the highest form of arrogance, even ignorance, to criticise the mission of another without having gone through the process of developing your own first. Yet, in seeking to spot the flaw first, the majority of people spend more time in knocking the ideals or missions of others, even of those they work with, with cynical remarks.

✝ Spending time developing a personal mission and understanding individual values, rather than criticising the suggestions of others over a charter of shared purpose, allows the alignment of individual values, beliefs and philosophy with a company. People who take the time to do this naturally view things from a different perspective. They may choose to leave, or they may choose to be proactive rather than reactive.

✸ The principle of putting your own house in order before complaining about the state of the street is a good one to follow. Just one person who genuinely cares about the direction of the company they work with can begin to make a significant difference, regardless of their station. People want meaning in their lives; the essential ingredient in success.

✸ Having and following a calling is exhilarating as it begins to permeate everything you do, shaping your actions and building your relationships. By creating and continually reviewing what you are about, what really absorbs and interests you, you ensure that you utilise your strengths to the full and perform to your best each day, a best that continually improves.

Guardian of Energy

✸ In the same way that we are capable of holding a desire because we have the inherent abilities to achieve it; each of us has a specific calling which our inherent strengths are perfectly designed to serve. That is the reason for our strengths, their very intent. Strengths, talents and natural skills, or lack of them, are expressions of the way our inner force manifests itself.

✶ Each of us is pure energy and it is our responsibility how we direct our energy. If we allow others to drain our energy, then we must accept responsibility for allowing it to happen. Similarly, whenever we involve ourselves in something that is of no interest to us, then we must be aware, as well as accept, that we are not utilising ourselves in a manner that will ever bring fulfilment.

✶ By focusing on what we can do, through being conscious of our strengths, by recognising those opportunities that appeal to us, by becoming a specialist in what we naturally excel in and are good at, and by following a calling that means the world to us, each of us will consciously, and unconsciously, gravitate to that which holds meaning for us and direct us in channelling our energy.

The tiger-cub howled as it limped home. 'I am never going to spring and jump again,' he complained to his father.

'But that is what you are naturally good at,' his father consoled, then playfully bowling over the young cub with his immensely powerful paw, added, 'Do you not enjoy it?'

'Not any more!' cried the cub. 'I put everything into that last jump and all I get is hurt for my trouble.'

'My son, you are a guardian of all the special strength and power that is contained within you. As guardian you must learn how to channel it, for such energy, when misdirected, will otherwise hurt you. Your energy has no limitations, other than the ones you allow it to have. Just because you have hurt yourself once or twice, in trying, does not mean that you will always do so. You must persevere.

'When you next spring and jump, first contain your energy, becoming aware of just how much you will need and why you are about to use it. As you do, you will feel the energy build up inside you until, when the moment feels just right, you let it go. At that moment you will experience your body, mind and energy flowing as one unit. Then you will no longer be jumping, you will be flying through the air. And the air itself will be with you, riding the tiger.'

*Continue the way of self-mastery
through individual inner understanding with:*

The Teachings of Billionaire Yen Tzu

Volume II